Self-discovery the Jungian way

Clearly and entertainingly written, *Self-Discovery the Jungian Way* presents an exciting new technique of self-analysis. Based on the psychological theories of C.G. Jung, the 'Watchword' technique will enable you to identify your psychological type and to explore the structure and dynamics of your personality. As you learn to recognize the various forces and tendencies within the psyche, you will acquire greater understanding of your inner self and your personal relationships.

This practical method of self-exploration guides you systematically along the difficult path towards the ultimate goal of self-realization or individuation. It uses a structured form of word association which you assess and interpret yourself, following simple guidelines that require no numerical scoring.

Easy to understand and fun to use, the book makes an intriguing and useful introductory guide to Jungian analytical psychology. It will appeal to a wide range of readers, including professional psychologists and students of psychology, counsellors and psychotherapists, as well as anyone interested in self-exploration and personal growth.

Michael Daniels is a chartered psychologist with a longstanding interest in Jungian psychology and self-actualization. He is Senior Lecturer in Psychology at Liverpool Polytechnic.

Self-discovery the Jungian way
The Watchword technique

Michael Daniels

London and New York

For my family

First published in 1992
by Routledge
11 New Fetter Lane, London EC4P 4EE

Simultaneously published in the USA and Canada
by Routledge
a division of Routledge, Chapman and Hall Inc.
29 West 35th Street, New York, NY 10001

© 1992 Michael Daniels

Typeset in Times Roman by Leaper & Gard Ltd, Bristol
Printed and bound in Great Britain by
Mackays of Chatham PLC, Chatham, Kent

British Library Cataloguing in Publication Data

Daniels, Michael *1950–*
   Self-discovery the Jungian way : the Watchword technique
   1. Self-development
   I. Title
   158.1

Library of Congress Cataloging in Publication Data also available

ISBN 0–415–07111–9
   0–415–06755–3 (pbk)

Contents

155.28
D186s

List of tables and figures		vi
Preface		vii
Acknowledgements		x
1	**Towards self-knowledge**	1
2	**The Watchword technique**	9
3	**Rationale and structure**	13
4	**The Watchword keys**	34
5	**Psychological types**	51
6	**The interpretive process**	90
7	**An example of self-analysis**	107
8	**Analysing change**	123
9	**Final thoughts**	133
	Appendix: blank matrix forms	138
	Bibliography	143
	Name index	145
	Subject index	146

Tables and figures

TABLES

1 The Watchword connections   11
2 The symbolism of up and down   17
3 The symbolism of left and right   23
4 Key principles and psychological indications   31
5 The sixteen Jungian psychological types   56
6 Examples of word associations   93
7 Key interpretations for Matrix 39 (Rachel)   96–7
8 The seven dialectical relationships   97
9 Stage 3: Word associations (Author, 1984)   110

FIGURES

1 Sequence of words and associations   10
2 Simple graphic symbols   16
3 The Greek cross   26
4 The cross of self-realization   27
5 The Watchword keys   29
6 The principal dimensions   29
7 Dimensional combinations   30
8 The balance/tension of inner and outer   30
9 The balance/tension of progression and regression   30
10 The final resolution   31
11 The functions of consciousness   53
12 The eight function types   54
13 The three developmental relationships   98
14 Comparison of the developmental models of Watchword and Jung   103

Preface

This book has been written with certain misgivings. Not least of these is the thought that surely we have enough publications already in the high street that claim to offer guidance for people seeking self-development, enlightenment, fulfilment, self-actualization, well-being, positive mental health, perfection, happiness, or whatever is the currently fashionable label for such things.

If the evidence in the bookshops is anything to go by, then there is no doubt – the 'New Age' is upon us with a vengeance and we run the very real risk of drowning in the flood of alternative literature. No longer is self-discovery the preserve of the philosopher, psychologist, religious initiate or eccentric amateur. In their own fashion, large numbers of quite ordinary people are expressing an extraordinary appetite for information and guidance in such matters. As a result, there has developed a ready, ever-expanding market for every conceivable interest and taste, from astrology to Zen Buddhism – and within each of these areas enough material, it would seem, to keep anyone busy for a lifetime.

Many people who have tried the *Watchword* technique have told me, however, that this is something not only quite new to them but, more importantly, both practical and accessible to the layperson who has no specialist knowledge of systems of self-development. Even those who at first do not learn much from the method generally find it interesting and intriguing, and they are often all too eager to try it out again – on their friends and acquaintances, as well as themselves. I have known occasions when the technique has travelled through a network of people and groups with the manner and speed of an infection. Consequently, I have been surprised on several occasions by strangers telling me that they have 'done' the exercise before.

Until now, although I have explained the basic technique and system to students, friends and others I have taught personally, no complete formal exposition of the method has been available. As a result, many have gone away either muddled or failing to understand fully the complexities of the system. This, I believe, has been a particular problem when the technique has been learned secondhand or at some further remove. For this reason, although I do not feel completely ready to go into print at this stage and would prefer the opportunity for further research, it is important that the basic system should be published now. In this way inaccuracies that might have arisen can be corrected immediately. This book is also a direct response to numerous requests I have received to write a simple yet detailed explanation of the Watchword system, together with a set of clear guidelines for the individual who wishes to use the technique and yet does not have the benefit of personal tuition.

Watchword has been described to me by one reviewer as a 'firmly orthodox Jungian technique', a description that I am happy and proud to endorse yet which, I feel, needs some explanation. Let me say at the outset that I am not a Jungian analyst. Although I have been interested in Carl Jung's analytical psychology since my early days as an undergraduate and have in recent years taught his system to many groups of students, I never viewed myself as a true 'Jungian' until I began to work with Watchword. My earlier interest and research in the concept of self-actualization approached this topic from the perspective of humanistic, developmental and existential psychology (e.g., Daniels, 1982, 1984, 1988). While I was aware of and fascinated by Jung's ideas, I always found his theories to be rather abstruse and difficult to apply to everyday life and experience.

Developing the Watchword system has involved me in a strange, almost mysterious process of intellectual discovery – even, I am tempted to say, revelation. As I studied and pondered the technique, I seemed to be drawn inexorably closer and closer towards a Jungian formulation. Time and again I found myself gazing disbelievingly at a quite unanticipated yet undeniable parallel between what my studies and research were revealing and some important element within Jung's theoretical approach. Of course my thinking must have been influenced by my prior reading of Jung, but this influence was essentially uncontrived. To give but one example: it was some considerable time after I had realized the basic structure of the Watchword matrix and related this to Jung's description of the process of *individuation* (in fact I had already begun preparing this book) that I suddenly saw his theory of psychological types staring up at me from the matrices I was then examining.

I say all this not to be inscrutable nor to tantalize the reader but to make quite clear that I did not start out with the intention of devising a specifically Jungian technique. In many respects I am as surprised as the next person may be that Watchword has turned out this way. It confirms in my mind, however, that there is something essentially true and basic in Jung's psychology.

Watchword is a practical technique that is designed to be used. In this regard it is one of the very few Jungian-based methods available either to professionals or to the general public for exploring an individual's psychological experience. In writing this book in as non-technical and relevant a way as I am able, it is my hope that Jungian psychology may become more widely known, understood, respected and, above all, employed. In addition to its primary use as a means by which any person may approach the task of self-exploration, Watchword will be of particular interest to Jungian analysts as well as to a wide range of therapists, counsellors and others who work with clients or peers in the general area of psychological health or personal growth.

This brief explanation will make clear that Watchword should not be viewed as having achieved a final state of development. Additional research is indicated and new discoveries may be anticipated. In offering Watchword to the judgement of a wider audience at this time, it is my hope that this may encourage much-needed independent assessments of the technique. In this respect I would welcome any communications from readers who feel they have observations, data or ideas that may be of value and interest. Please write to Michael Daniels, Centre for Psychology, The Liverpool Polytechnic, Trueman Street Building, 15–21 Webster Street, Liverpool, L3 2ET, UK. I regret, however, that I am unable to enter into correspondence regarding the interpretation of individual matrices.

This book is designed to be read sequentially. If, however, you wish to try out the Watchword technique immediately then you should turn straight to Chapter 2.

Acknowledgements

I wish to express my thanks to: the unknown originator of the proto-technique that provided the foundation for the Watchword system; Brian Lancaster for starting me off on this quest; my wife for her patience, care and judgement; finally, and especially, all the people who have kindly allowed me to examine their matrices and to explore their psychological life.

1 Towards self-knowledge

'Know thyself', Socrates urges us, for 'the unexamined life is not worth living'. Throughout history and across the cultural divide, self-knowledge has been recognized as a major – perhaps the major – mark of the truly mature, enlightened person and, simultaneously, as a royal road to ultimate fulfilment.

CURIOSITY AND ENTERTAINMENT

Most people, if asked, would readily accept the importance of self-understanding. Furthermore, if the current fashion for the kind of 'test-yourself' questionnaires found in popular magazines is anything to go by, it would seem that many of us have an almost insatiable curiosity to discover unknown 'facts' about ourselves – our latent talents, secret longings, sexual attractiveness, basic values, emotional needs, intellectual capacity, and so on. Much of this interest, I am sure, is motivated by a simple desire to be amused and flattered rather than by any genuine attempt to discover the 'truth' about our personalities or situations. Yet somewhere, at the back of our minds perhaps, there may be the vague, unvoiced hope that we might learn something of value.

Of course, the 'tests' that appear in the popular press have been designed primarily for their entertainment value and for their supposed ability to increase sales, not for their psychological validity. They are not intended to be taken too seriously by the reader, nor to make any lasting contribution to human knowledge. They are cultural ephemera to be enjoyed in an idle moment, discussed over a coffee break, and disposed of and forgotten by the next morning. For this reason, they have rarely been constructed in any rigorous manner and it is unusual for their results to have been assessed for accuracy. Put simply, you cannot be sure that what the test indicates about you is in any way true (although test results, like newspaper horoscopes, are often so general that they may apply to almost anyone).

PSYCHOLOGICAL MEASUREMENT

In contrast to the kind of questionnaires mentioned above (which are usually devised by journalists) the psychological profession has, over the years, developed a whole barrage of 'standardized' tests and assessment procedures for measuring everything from academic aptitude to zenophobia, adjustment to zestfulness. These tests have generally been constructed and evaluated according to accepted 'scientific' principles and as such they may be expected to produce data which describe faithfully the characteristics being assessed.

Unfortunately, the sheer number and bewildering variety of available tests make it impossible in practice for laypersons to make any sensible decisions about what ought to be measured in their particular cases. Even the average psychologist often finds difficulty in selecting tests for specific purposes and may need to consult colleagues with greater experience. More importantly, most psychological tests are complex or highly technical and usually require specialist training in administration, scoring and interpretation if they are to be used with any degree of confidence. For this reason, and because test results can be abused by the unscrupulous or inexperienced, the use of many psychological procedures is restricted to properly qualified individuals who agree to be bound by professional codes of conduct.

Many psychologists now offer assessment facilities on a commercial basis to both individuals and organizations. You may also have come across various agencies that will draw up personal profiles of skills, aptitudes, personality traits, needs or values. Generally this is done for the purpose of vocational guidance, personnel selection or management training, and in these terms bona fide psychologists and agencies can provide a valuable service.

THE LIMITATIONS OF PSYCHOLOGICAL TESTS

Although it will often be found interesting and helpful to obtain such a psychological profile, there are also very real personal dangers in this kind of objective description of the self. Most importantly, we may come to believe that our personality is fixed and unalterable; that we will always be intelligent, popular or anxious, for example, because we 'possess' these particular qualities. Secondly, such characterization leads us subtly into thinking of ourselves as just a collection of unrelated psychological components. This belief inevitably takes away from us the sense of unity and wholeness that is the cornerstone of our experience of being persons. Psychological tests may point out the trees, but what about the wood? Where am 'I' in all this complex description of 'attributes'?

More than this, psychological tests don't *explain* anything; they cannot indicate meaning, context or personal significance. It may or may not be interesting to learn that I have a high anxiety level. But why am I anxious? What led to these feelings? What does my anxiety mean to me? What does it signify in the context of my present situation? What can or should I do about it? These are questions that remain unanswered from test results for they are indeed unanswerable in this manner.

If I may be permitted an analogy that is, perhaps, not as trite as it may at first appear, the psychological measurement of a person is rather like describing a book by listing its subject matter and literary qualities. Thus the book is an historical novel set in the Victorian era, written in English, intelligently constructed, fascinating, insightful, factually accurate – overall a good read. Such a description is, of course, useful up to a point. It may, for example, help us to decide whether or not to buy it as a present for a friend. But it is no substitute for reading the book. It gives us no idea of the book's story, meaning or ultimate significance. In the final analysis, it is simply irrelevant.

The plain fact is that psychological tests have been designed by psychologists for psychologists (and for their paymasters) and that the purpose of the vast majority of these tests is to categorize and label *other people* so that their objective characteristics may be studied 'scientifically' and so that individuals may be assigned appropriate social roles or placed in their 'rightful' societal position. Even where tests are used diagnostically, for example in clinical or educational settings, their purpose is generally to justify and direct some kind of professional therapeutic intervention. In these cases it is more important that the psychologist can interpret and act on the results than that the client may gain insight into his or her own behaviour. With very few exceptions, psychological tests have not been developed as aids to self-understanding and their suitability for this purpose is therefore severely limited.

To continue the analogy used above, psychological tests describe people as a bookseller or librarian might describe a book. As such these descriptions are very useful for those in the business of buying, selling or cataloguing. But booksellers and librarians rarely read the volumes on their shelves and they certainly don't need to understand them in order to do their job properly. Psychologists with test batteries are not so very different.

THE NEED FOR UNDERSTANDING

Very few of us would claim that we could understand another person, whether a friend or a character in a novel for that matter, by being shown their psychological 'profile' – and we should not be hoodwinked into believing that self-understanding may be acquired in this way. Like characters in novels, real people can be truly understood only by appreciating the story of their lives. This is why we prefer to read the full narrative of a novel or biography or, failing that, an accurate synopsis. We would feel totally cheated and frustrated if the book or synopsis merely contained a set of test scores for each of the story's principal players. To know people is to know what has happened to them, what they are experiencing and doing now, and what they anticipate for the future. More than this, we need to understand how past, present and future are linked in a coherent and believable narrative unity. To do this we must *interpret* their lives. We must make sense of their actions and words. We must create a meaning that might eventually place everything into perspective.

The process of coming to know ourselves is, I believe, essentially the same. We must discover or, more accurately, continually re-*create* the story of our own lives – the pattern and meaning that can make sense of our individual journey. Such a story not only maps out past progress and enables us to take current bearings, but it may also indicate the way forward. In this manner our personal narrative provides a sense of direction, with positive guidance for the future, as well as offering an interpretation of past and present events.

LEARNING TO OBSERVE THE SELF

To begin our process of self-discovery we need to do two things. Firstly, we must learn to pay attention to our own situation, experience, thoughts, feelings and actions. Secondly, we must look for underlying patterns, structures and meanings. Although we may attempt these activities unaided, history teaches us that people have always sought external assistance of one kind or another. This has typically taken the form of learning special techniques of attentional training or self-examination (e.g., meditation, the keeping of diaries, free association, dream recall) usually combined with a particular system of psychological or psychospiritual interpretation (e.g., the Hebrew Cabala, Buddhist Abidharma, Freudian or Jungian psychoanalysis). Often such training takes place under the personal guidance of a teacher, guru, mentor, counsellor or therapist.

The reasons for this reliance on external aid are complex. Most crucially, it seems that people need to be taught how to observe themselves effectively. In any other branch of knowledge it is axiomatic that students must first learn basic observation skills. Fledgling geologists must be taught how to observe rock and soil, painters and photographers how to view a scene, physicians how to examine their patients, counsellors and therapists how to listen to their clients. We all know and take for granted the difference that a trained eye or ear can make in these areas.

When it comes to self-observation, however, most of us rather arrogantly and naively assume that we are naturally qualified. Perhaps this is because we feel we have some kind of immediate and direct access to the contents of our own minds – access that is denied to others and therefore something with which they cannot help us. Yet a moment's thought will reveal the fallacy of this view. In the first place we must all have surely experienced occasions when another person has shown greater insight into our personality or situation than we were immediately capable of. Secondly, of course, most of the time we don't observe ourselves at all – and certainly not in any rigorous or systematic fashion. We go through life largely on auto-pilot, only partially conscious and rarely in any sense truly *self*-conscious. We say, do and think things blithely, spontaneously, with little forethought and less reflection. We are, as Gurdjieff (1974) put it, to all intents 'asleep'; shaken briefly into wakefulness only on rare occasions of shock or personal trauma.

SCHOOLS AND SYSTEMS

Whenever we wake up sufficiently to take the process of self-observation seriously, we will immediately encounter further difficulties. One problem is that of knowing exactly what to observe. Clearly we cannot attend to everything that we experience and do and, like our trainee geologists and painters, we must learn to notice what is important and to ignore irrelevant details.

In practice, what we are taught to observe depends critically upon the particular school or system of self-understanding that we follow. For example, Buddhists will be taught to pay attention, via their meditation practice, to bodily sensations and to the spontaneous flow of disconnected thoughts as they arise and disappear in consciousness. Gestalt therapists train their clients to recognize their emotions and to focus upon 'here and now' events. Freudian psychoanalysts encourage patients to 'free associate' (saying everything that comes into the mind without censoring thoughts in any way) and to talk freely about past experiences. Jungian analysts often emphasize the remembering and interpretation of dreams. Transactional analysis involves a system for examining patterns of communication between people. Rational-emotive therapy forces individuals to recognize and question the irrational beliefs that they hold about themselves and others. Whichever system is followed, a common denominator of all these 'insight' therapies is that people are taught to pay attention to some aspect of their being that they had previously been unable, unwilling, or simply too lazy to observe. The major differences between the various techniques are primarily a consequence of each method adopting its own theoretical perspective or interpretive system.

I do not wish to get involved in arguments about which procedure, perspective or system is 'best'. All have their advocates and devotees, and all can produce strings of clients who will swear to the success of the approach in their own particular cases. For what it is worth, the available objective evidence, based on comparisons of various forms of psycho-therapy, indicates that all methods are reasonably effective and that no one method is consistently better than any other (see, for example, Rachman and Wilson, 1980; Smith *et al.*, 1980). There is also some indication that the effectiveness of an approach depends partly upon the nature of the problems a person has and also upon individual temperament or character. What this evidence clearly suggests, however, is that some form of self-examination is certainly better than none.

SELF-DECEPTION AND THE ROLE OF THE OTHER

No matter which technique of self-observation is adopted, a problem that is always faced is that of bias or self-deception. Most of us like to think well of ourselves and it is all too easy to allow our personal vanity and need for esteem to distort the evidence of our senses. In this way we all show a tendency to 'cook the books' so that we are revealed, for example, to be warm, good, popular, consistent or untroubled (a few people, however, have such a low opinion of themselves that they may unrealistically emphasize their bad qualities).

One of the main arguments in favour of employing a teacher or therapist is that it is often much harder to fool someone else than it is to deceive ourselves. Because of this, such people may, if they are doing their job properly, act as a faithful mirror to the self, helping to reveal us to ourselves in our true light and colours. This is important because experience shows that the process of self-study, when working effectively, generally throws up much highly unpleasant material about the self. For the simple fact is that we are almost certainly not as good, consistent or untroubled as we may care to think and once we start digging into the self we can unearth some messy stuff indeed. Most people's response to this, rather than working with and learning from the experience, is either to turn a blind eye or to become overwhelmed by feelings of guilt, shame or personal failure. Here a teacher or therapist can help enormously by encouraging us to keep things in proper perspective and by suggesting ways of making sense of it all.

A related reason for working with another is the ability of an independent mind to confront and challenge the self, providing a much-needed stimulus to personal growth. In the absence of this kind of challenge it is easy to avoid paying attention to personal problems that ideally should be worked upon. Also we allow ourselves to continue through life unchanged, with our old, habitual, often stereotyped and unhelpful attitudes intact.

PARTIAL METHODS

Many people have no desire to follow a prolonged course of intense personal discipline or individual therapy. Or they may simply not have the time, opportunity or resources to further their interest. Such people usually rely on other external aids to self-understanding such as books, workshops or short courses in order to give them basic ideas and practical material which they may then utilize in their own time as they see fit.

The last decade has seen a burgeoning of interest in this approach to self-discovery. This is witnessed, for example, by the huge growth in the number of books published each year on various techniques of self-development such as meditation, dream analysis, auto-hypnosis, positive thinking, the I Ching and creative visualization. Then again there are innumerable courses and workshops being offered in every major city on such things as assertiveness training, co-counselling, encounter, dance therapy, psychodrama or Reichian massage. Endless variety here for all interests, tastes and pockets.

Provided these methods are approached with a degree of care, discrimination, objectivity and, not least, humour, there is much of value that can be learned. In the absence of these qualities, it must also be said that there are definite associated hazards. In addition to the problem of self-deception, there is the more immediate danger of rushing headlong into activities that may serve no useful purpose in our particular case. It is sad to report that many people, failing to realize any clear overall strategy for self-development, become addicted to these techniques, either sticking rigidly and dogmatically to a chosen favourite or jumping wildly from one to another in a seemingly desperate search for new experience or new 'truths' about the self. But the very nature of most of these activities is that they provide partial answers to circumscribed problems. They are not panaceas for every ill, nor are they intended to become crutches upon which people become dependent. Above all, they are not religions or ideologies. They should be approached cautiously and intelligently, used only when appropriate, and abandoned as soon as they have outlived their purpose.

The major limitation of these partial techniques is that they fail to provide any overall picture of the self and its narrative history. Because of this they cannot serve to guide our lives in any meaningful fashion. They may provide helpful short-term relief and practical assistance in specific situations, but even then only when we have decided that this is what our life's story requires of us at this moment in time. But how do we make these decisions? How do we discover our self's story? What 'method' can help us in our quest for meaning and personal significance?

One answer to these questions is undoubtedly the process of working with another, as exemplified in genuine spiritual traditions by the dialogue between teacher and student and in counselling or psychotherapy by that between therapist and client. But what can the individual seeker do? Is there nothing that those who prefer to go it alone can use to aid their attempts at understanding the whole pattern of their lives?

THE WATCHWORD TECHNIQUE

It is against this background that the Watchword technique is set. Watchword is, in one sense, a 'partial' method of self-discovery. Certainly the technique is not something that should come to be relied upon or taken too seriously. It is not the only tool of self-discovery an individual may need, nor necessarily the best, nor indispensable. But in focusing upon the whole of the self, in stimulating self-questioning and inner dialogue, and in providing a means of interpreting the self's development as well as structure, Watchword offers the promise that we may begin to decipher our own personal mystery – the story of our life.

A beginning. A tool. This is all that is claimed. The work, the achievement, the meaning – all these will be your own. Try out the technique. Learn from it if you can. Dismiss it if you must. But give it a fair trial. At the very least you should find the experience interesting.

2 The Watchword technique

It is instructive to gain one's first experience of the Watchword technique while innocent of its exact purpose and, more particularly, its structure. For this reason, try to resist the temptation to skim through the remainder of the book at this stage. Just read on and follow the simple set of procedures outlined below. If you have been told something about the technique by a friend or have already glanced at some of the pages, that can't be helped. You may decide later how much your prior knowledge has influenced what you are about to do. But so that others may approach Watchword spontaneously, please don't bias the expectations of your friends by revealing the technique's system before they have the chance of completing at least one exercise. In the long run they will thank you for your silence.

COMPLETING THE WATCHWORD MATRIX

To begin, all you need to know is that Watchword is a game of word association. Make sure that you are comfortable and will not be disturbed for at least half an hour. You may wish to take the telephone off the hook. Ideally you should be alone but, in any case, do not allow anyone to watch or comment upon what you are doing, or to interfere in any other way.

Now try to clear your mind of any current preoccupations. Close your eyes and focus gently on the sensations of breathing slowly in and out. Relax any obvious tensions in your body, adjusting your position if necessary. You should be aiming to achieve a state of relaxed, vacant attentiveness. Try to forget what you are about to do. Above all, if you have carried out the Watchword technique before, avoid rehearsing any responses you may think to make. Simply pay attention to your breathing. Just two or three minutes in this kind of mental preparation will be found more than to repay the time spent.

When you feel ready, take a copy of a blank matrix form (see Appendix) and proceed as follows:

Step 1

Place the form horizontally and write *eight different words*, from left to right, in the boxes along the *top* of the sheet. You may write any words at all – just the first words that come into your head. Try not to censor your thoughts in any way and don't spend too long thinking what to write. Also, don't write a sentence or grammatically connected sequence. Simply write eight separate words.

Step 2

Write another *eight different words*, from left to right, in the boxes along the *bottom* of the sheet. *Do not turn the sheet upside down to do this.* Again, just write the first words that come into your mind.

Step 3

Refer to Figure 1 and consider the two words that you have written in boxes 1 and 2. Now think of another word that, in your opinion, *somehow connects* the two words that you are considering. The connection can be of any kind at all as long as it makes sense to you. Don't worry if another person might not understand the association you make. If you think of more than one connecting word, choose the one that provides the link

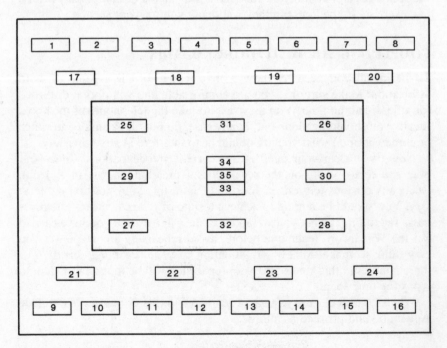

Figure 1 Sequence of words and associations

Table 1 The Watchword connections

Boxes to connect		Connecting box
1	2	17
3	4	18
5	6	19
7	8	20
9	10	21
11	12	22
13	14	23
15	16	24
17	18	25
19	20	26
21	22	27
23	24	28
25	27	29
26	28	30
25	26	31
27	28	32
29	30	33
31	32	34
33	34	35

which, in your opinion, is the most personally meaningful. The word you choose must be different from the two you are considering but it may, if so desired, be the same as a word written elsewhere on the sheet. If you cannot think of a *single* word that makes an appropriate link, you may use a short phrase instead. Now write the connecting word (phrase) in box 17.

Step 4

Repeat Step 3, using the sequence of connections shown in Table 1. Do not run ahead of yourself – make sure that each connection is written down before proceeding to the next. Also, once you have written a connecting word, do not change it.

QUESTIONS

You have now completed the basic Watchword procedure and are ready to begin to interpret what you have done. Before reading further, however, you might like to consider these questions:

1 Did you feel that, as you progressed through the exercise, you seemed to be tapping deeper and more psychologically meaningful layers of thought?

2 Do the eleven words that appear within the rectangular outline seem in

any way significant to you, perhaps when understood as metaphors or symbols?

3 Do the central three words in particular seem to encapsulate or symbol- ize something very basic about your personality or present situation?

If you can answer 'yes' to these questions, then you should find the interpretive process interesting, relatively straightforward and, hopefully, informative. If, on the other hand, the words you have written seem trivial or meaningless, this does not necessarily indicate that the exercise has not 'worked' for you. It may mean, however, that the process of interpretation will require some effort on your part and a willingness to explore indirect or symbolic associations.

3 Rationale and structure

THE DEVELOPMENT OF WATCHWORD

In 1984, a psychologist colleague showed me a simple technique of word association that he had himself been taught by a friend. He didn't know quite how or where this technique had originated and subsequent enquiries have failed to identify a specific source, but it seems that the basic method had been doing the rounds for several years, being passed on from one interested person to another. The purpose of this technique was to trace a sequence of associations from an original set of sixteen freely generated words until a single resultant connection was formed. This final word was believed to be of some important personal significance.

The technique intrigued me, as it seemed clearly the case that the word I had derived expressed something essential about my situation at the time. More than this, however, I felt that many of the other connecting words I had formed were also personally significant and, crucially, that they were organized according to some distinct underlying pattern or structure.

For many months I speculated upon and experimented with the technique, using myself and friends as guinea pigs. In studying the results, organizational principles gradually began to emerge and the basic structure of the Watchword matrix became established. Through my experiments and deliberations I also found it useful to extend much further the sequence of connections that I had originally been shown. Finally, as I have explained in the Preface, in developing the Watchword structure I found myself being drawn inexorably towards the specifically Jungian formulation that will be described. In this respect I repeat that Watchword may be considered to be one of the very few truly Jungian techniques of self-analysis that are available for general use.

Since evolving the Watchword system I have demonstrated the technique to several hundred people, both individually and in groups. Many of these have also been interested enough to try the basic method with their own families, friends or colleagues. It is very difficult to test scientifically a procedure such as Watchword, although preliminary studies on the kinds of connections made have given support to the system's basic structure. I can say with confidence, however, that most people who have tried the method and have examined their responses carefully find Watchword to be both interesting and enlightening. In many cases individuals have been astounded at the accuracy of Watchword's personal diagnosis and have gained important practical insights into their present situations.

WATCHWORD'S PURPOSE

Watchword is an aid to psychological understanding. Its purpose is to help individuals to identify important psychological forces and tendencies operating within their own beings so that they may begin to understand more clearly their own personal stories. Unlike astrology, the I Ching, tarot and similar divinational practices, Watchword is not a system of fortune telling and it does not directly offer advice about problems. In providing a description and interpretation of the psychological 'field' in which a person is currently operating it may, however, assist the making of choices and decisions.

In a very real sense, *you* are accountable for everything that the Watchword technique generates. You choose each word and every association, and you decide how to interpret the series of connections that you have made. The structure of the Watchword matrix, to be described later, is intended to provide merely a skeleton of possible meanings upon which you must hang the flesh of your own experience. With Watchword, you become your own analyst. This book should provide all the information you need and it is not necessary to consult a guru, therapist or expert. While you may find it useful to discuss your matrices with others, you should exercise caution in permitting anyone else to suggest interpretations. If nothing else, Watchword is a useful technique for teaching us to trust our own insights and intuitions.

At one level, Watchword may be considered simply as an amusing party game or form of psychological solitaire. At its most profound, it is a system that may be used to guide the individual along the path towards self-fulfilment. In the terminology of Carl Jung's analytical psychology, the Watchword matrix provides a *uniting symbol* or representation of the whole integrated *psyche*, mind or personality (see, for example, Jacobi, 1968; Jung, 1968a, b, c). Jung believed that by studying and reflecting upon such uniting symbols, which are generally symmetrical images arranged about a central point (for example the Hindu and Buddhist *mandalas*), the person was aided in the difficult process of self-realization or *individuation*. These symbols do not simply describe psychological harmony; they may, according to Jung, help a person to achieve it.

STRUCTURAL PRINCIPLES

Like typical mandala symbols (see, for example, Jung, 1968a; Tucci, 1961) the Watchword matrix takes the form of a square (or circle), symbolizing wholeness, in which there is special emphasis on the centre, representing the point of union or balance of opposites. For purposes of interpretation, the Watchword 'square' is made up of the eight words around the inner sides of the main rectangle. The 'centre' comprises the three central words, of which the final (middle) word provides the ultimate focus.

In addition to the relationship between a centre and its circumference, Watchword's interpretive structure utilizes the concept of *spatial metaphor*. Put simply, this means that space or, more particularly, *direction* within space relative to an observer has important symbolic associations. Like most mandala symbols, the Watchword matrix is based upon the *principle of four*, represented by the four directions in which an object may move on a two-dimensional surface – i.e., forward, backward, left and right. Because of the way that the matrix is constructed on the page, forward and backward are indicated by top (up) and bottom (down).

THE VERTICAL DIMENSION

The concepts of 'up' (top, high) and 'down' (bottom, low), in addition to indicating relative spatial position, have a number of connotative associations that are fairly universal. When we feel good, happy and full of energy, we say that we are *up*, on *top* form, or on *top* of the world. In contrast, when we feel poorly, sad, apathetic or sluggish we say that we are *low*, run *down*, *down* in the mouth, or *down* in the dumps. In these circumstances we may be admonished to buck *up* or wake *up*. We aim *high*, lie *low*, *climb* the ladder to success, *fall* from grace or favour, *raise* a laugh, *lower* our standards, *rise* above temporary difficulties, or *sink* into *depths* of depravity. To mature is to grow *up*, whereas in old age we enter a physical and mental *decline*. Cultivated people are *high*brow. The vulgar and coarse are *low*. College dons sit at *high* table while errant students are sent *down*. It is '*up* with' our own team and '*down* with' the opposition.

Throughout history, high places such as mountain tops have been associated with the elevation of the spirit, with ecstatic or 'peak' experiences, and with communion with God. Low, subterranean places, such as caverns, pits, mines and vaults are generally associated with evil, joylessness, corruption or death. In Greek mythology, for example, Mount Olympus is the abode of the Gods. The dead, on the other hand, along with many evils such as old age and disease, live in the Underworld, in eternal gloom, dampness and silence. In Christian belief, heaven is usually believed to be 'up there'. Perhaps it is fondly pictured as being a realm of love and beauty somewhere above the clouds. Certainly it is the place to which souls *ascend*. In contrast, the damned are believed to descend into hell – often represented as a region of choking fire and sulphur, deep underground. Angels, spirits, sylphs, fairies and similarly benevolent mythical creatures are usually winged, symbolizing flight and rising above earthly constraints. Such beings are clearly differentiated from monsters, ogres, trolls, gnomes – bogeys of all sorts – who traditionally live under-ground or in caves. Satan, it may be noted, is also known as the angel of the bottomless pit.

Objects or structures that are vertical generally symbolize movement up or down levels of moral or spiritual being. Often they indicate a bridge between one world and another. Perhaps the most ancient of these symbols is that of the sacred tree found in many myths and religions (e.g., the biblical tree of the knowledge of good and evil, the Norse Yggdrasil or world tree, the tree of life of the Cabalists). With its roots far underground and its leaves and branches thrusting to the sky, the tree indicates a connection or pathway between the lower and upper worlds. This connec-tion passes through the middle world of human experience, represented by the trunk. By climbing this trunk it is believed that ordinary mortals may ascend to the realm of the Gods. This idea of moral or spiritual elevation through human effort is also inherent in the symbolism of the beanstalk, ladder, tower, staircase, rope, stake, pole, mast, hill and pyramid – gener-ally anything that reaches vertically from the ground towards the sky.

In the human body, it is the vertical spinal column that represents the idea of moral progress or spiritual ascent. In connecting 'base' functions (excretion, sexuality) with the 'higher' intellectual or spiritual being (identi-fied with the head or brain) the spinal column becomes a symbol of transcendence or transmutation. It is no coincidence that ancient religions often refer to the backbone as a road, ladder or tree.

Perhaps the most elaborate example of spinal symbolism is that of *kundalini yoga* (see, for example, Wood, 1962). In this doctrine a divine energy, known as the *kundalini*, is believed to lie dormant at the base of the spine (usually it is pictured as a coiled, sleeping snake). Through correct yogic practice, over many years, the kundalini may allegedly be

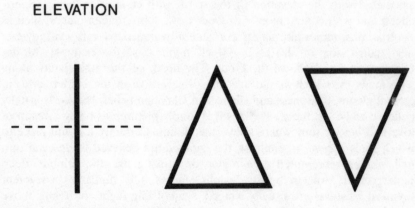

DYNAMISM   EVOLUTION   INVOLUTION
ELEVATION

Figure 2 Simple graphic symbols

Table 2 The symbolism of up and down

Up	Down
Progression	Regression
Superior	Inferior
Dynamic	Static
Energetic	Apathetic
Ascent	Descent
Evolution	Involution
Forward	Backward
Future	Past
Mature	Immature
Happy	Sad
Good	Evil
Moral	Immoral
Heaven	Hell
Spiritual	Material
Refined	Gross
Life	Death
Growth	Decay
Health	Illness

aroused, made erect and caused to ascend a channel of energy inside the spinal column. As the kundalini passes through various psychic centres, or *chakras*, new awareness and enhanced powers are supposedly acquired. Eventually, when the kundalini reaches the highest chakra, the 'thousand petalled lotus' situated in the brain, the yogi is believed to achieve oneness with the universe.

Many glyphs and graphic signs also symbolize the notion of energy, development or elevation. The simplest of these is just a vertical line – usually incorporated into more complex signs such as the cross. More sophisticated ideas can be indicated by the triangle. When it points upwards, the triangle symbolizes spirituality, progression or evolution. Pointing downwards, it represents evil, regression or involution (cf. Cirlot, 1971). In this context it may be noted that an important part of the symbolism of the pyramid derives from its triangular, upward-pointing faces.

From all this evidence it seems that the vertical dimension typically expresses the ideas of energy, level, progress, morality and spirituality. The two poles of the dimension (up-top-high vs down-bottom-low) thus encapsulate a series of dichotomies that relate clearly to these basic ideas. These dichotomies are summarized in Table 2.

THE HORIZONTAL DIMENSION: FIRST CONSIDERATIONS

In a similar but much less obvious way, the directions left and right also have symbolic meanings that have been recognized, for example, in many religions and mythologies. Interestingly, as we shall see, many of these traditional associations have in recent years gained considerable support from what may seem the most unlikely of sources – neuropsychological studies of human brain function.

Nowadays the primary and most salient distinctions between the meanings of left and right are as follows:

Left = weak, false, impure, abnormal, disordered, taboo.
Right = strong, correct, pure, normal, ordered, permitted.

Derogation of the left and left-handedness may be traced in all languages of the Indo-European family, as well as many others. The English word 'left' comes from the Old English 'lyft', meaning weak or worthless. 'Sinister' is simply Latin for the left side. The French '*gauche*' (left) also means naive, crude or awkward, while the Italian '*mancino*' means not only left-handed but also treacherous, dishonest, crooked or maimed. If further evidence is necessary, the *Oxford English Dictionary* includes the following among the meanings of left or left-handed: mean, ill-omened, inauspicious, underhand, inferior, crippled, defective, awkward, clumsy, ambiguous, doubtful and spurious.

In direct contrast, the right side indicates 'right' in every sense (e.g., correct, true, straight, proper, standard, orthodox, normal, whole, sound, righteous, just, lawful). The right is also forthright, upright, downright and outright. To 'put right' is to recover or mend. The right-hand side is the position of honour or precedence and an invaluable assistant is a 'right-hand man'. We greet each other, salute, make the sign of the cross and swear oaths with our right hand – and to be right-handed is to be skilful, dextrous (Lat. '*dexter*' = right) and adroit (Fr. '*droit*' = right).

THE QUESTION OF HANDEDNESS

Perhaps the simplest explanation that has been offered for these differences in meaning is the predominance of right-handedness in all modern-day cultures (left-handers consistently make up only about 5 to 10 per cent of the adult population). Studies of prehistoric art and artefacts indicate a similar favouring of the right hand dating back at least 5,000 years and possibly much further. Thus for the vast majority of people the right hand is, and may always have been, the strongest and most coordinated. Being in this majority, right-handers understandably assume that this is the natural, normal, good or correct pattern. Their own awkwardness when using the left hand, coupled with the left-hander's apparent clumsiness on many tasks, has led to an inevitable belief in the superiority and 'rightness' of the *don't swallow this ₱ whole*

right. Combine this with suggestions that left-handedness is associated with epilepsy, dyslexia, stuttering, learning difficulties, emotional disturbance and homosexuality (cf. Annett, 1985; Barsley, 1966, 1970) and it is easy to see how the left comes to symbolize abnormality, evil and degeneracy.

Appealing though this explanation may be, there are certain problems with it. Firstly, the evidence that right-handedness is 'natural' (i.e., inherited or biologically based) is rather weak. Humans are, for example, alone among the primates in showing a consistent favouring of the right hand. Although individuals in other primate species often show a preference for one hand or the other, left-handedness is just as common as right-handedness. Furthermore, human infants use both hands with equal facility. After developing through a series of stages in which the right and left hands may be alternately favoured, one hand eventually begins to dominate. Distinct handedness does not become fixed, however, until about the age of eight (Gesell and Ames, 1947).

This pattern of development may, of course, reflect biologically based processes of physical maturation. Alternatively, the child may simply be *learning* to use one hand (generally the right). In this context it should be remembered that although we tend to define handedness in terms of the hand that we write with, many people prefer to use their other hand (or foot) for certain activities. We are all, to some degree, mixed-handed or ambidextrous.

As if confirming the role of learning in the development of handedness is the very obvious evidence (obvious, that is, to left-handers) that most cultures go out of their way actively to discourage and suppress left-handedness. This occurs not only in subtle ways such as in the design of scissors, fountain pens, sewing machines and golf clubs but also through deliberate attempts by parents and teachers to force children to use their right hands. In some cases it has been reported that children's left arms have been bandaged so that they could not be used. If right-handedness is really so natural, it is argued, why should such extreme measures be necessary?

If right-handedness is learned, we are faced with the conclusion that right is good (strong, true, correct, normal, etc.) not because we are naturally right-handed; rather we are taught to be right-handed because right is seen to be good. There is, in other words, a *cultural* bias in favour of the right hand. This begs the question, however, why is right also good?

SOLAR AND LUNAR CULTS

Michael Barsley (1970) has suggested, and I am inclined to agree with him, that the prejudice against the left and left-handedness goes back to the rise of sun worship, a cult found among many ancient civilizations and peoples, including the Aryans, Assyrians, Persians, Egyptians, Greeks, Romans, North American Indians, Incas and Mayas. For people living in the northern hemisphere (and the vast majority of humankind still occupies this hemisphere) the sun's apparent movement is always clockwise (i.e., to the right). Furthermore, in facing north, the east (sunrise) is on the right; the west (sunset) is on the left. But why, you ask, should one face north in the first place?

Ancient man faced north in two senses. Firstly, there is evidence that the earliest migrations of the human species were northward, from central to north Africa, and from there into Europe and Asia. On these prehistoric migrations, the sun would have risen on the right and set on the left. Such a coincidence must surely have imprinted itself powerfully upon the human psyche in the course of its long evolution. Secondly, in the northern hemisphere, the obvious and only fixed point of reference from which bearings may be taken is the Pole Star, or North Star. In support of this suggestion is the evidence that in the myths of many peoples this star is held in particular esteem precisely because it is seen to be the place about which the heavens turn.

Understood in this way, it is easy to see how right and left acquire certain symbolic associations. Thus right (east), being the direction of sunrise, carries with it the promise of day – light, warmth, awakening, regeneration, activity, knowledge and beauty. In contrast, left (west), the direction of sunset, indicates the onset of night – darkness, coldness, fear, unconsciousness, fatigue, mystery and illusion.

In the context of a solar cult, sunrise (the right) also becomes a symbol of spiritual illumination and the encounter with God, whereas sunset (at the left hand) comes to symbolize God's abandonment of His people or His defeat by the forces of anarchy and evil. Thus we may understand why it is that, according to St Matthew's Gospel, on the Day of Judgement the sheep will sit on the right hand of God, the goats on the left. It is for these reasons also that Greek and Roman temples generally opened towards the east, while Christian churches have the altar at the east end. In contrast, since prehistoric times corpses have often been buried with their heads turned to the west – the traditional abode of the dead. In Greek mythology, the principal entrance to the Underworld was to be found in the far west and even today we speak of people or things having 'gone west' when we mean they have died, become lost or made useless.

As the sun 'dies' in the west, it is replaced in the heavens by the 'Queen of the Night', the moon. In this way the west (left) also comes to acquire lunar associations (the moon is not linked with the east because it is seldom seen to rise). Since earliest times, the moon has been associated with the mysterious processes of nature (e.g., tides, rains, seasons, life and death, fertility, decay, sexuality), with human mysteries and inner workings (sleep, dreaming, imagination, instincts, emotions, illness, madness, fortune, magic) and, in particular, with the mysteries of women (e.g., menstruation, conception, pregnancy, childbirth). Many of these associations are based upon simple observations of (or analogies with) the nature and effects of lunar cycles.

The moon's influence on tides has long been recognized. Many peoples also link the moon's phases to rainfall, to the growth of vegetation and to the behaviour of animals, especially sea creatures. The earliest calendars were based on the lunar month of about 28 days, with the passing of time being reckoned in 'moons'. Lunar calendars were first used among nomadic tribes to track the seasonal migrations of the herd. With the development of a settled village agriculture, the lunar calendar was used to regulate the cycles of planting and harvesting and also to calculate the timing of religious celebrations. Even today several religions use the lunar calendar to determine their festivals.

Being associated with night, the relationship of the moon to sleep and dreaming (and hence imagination) is obvious. The supposed influence of the moon on human emotions and moods and its link with madness (lunacy) are part of our folklore. The moon's waxing and waning also suggest parallels with health and illness, with birth and death, and with the vagaries of human fortune, while its ever-changing shape is a powerful symbol of magical transformation.

Perhaps the most important aspect of lunar symbolism derives from the moon's supposed relationship with women. The moon is considered to be female in most mythologies. Even when the moon is male, his function is generally seen as the impregnation of women. Without doubt this association with women is based upon the remarkable coincidence between the approximately 28-day lunar and menstrual cycles. Not only does the word 'menstruation' come from the Latin *'mensis'* (month) but statistical evidence is also claimed that links women's cycles with the moon's phases (see Jongbloet, 1983). In many beliefs, women may regularize their periods by exposing their bodies to the moon's rays, or they may utilize the phases of the moon as a primitive method of birth control. The waxing of the moon also suggests a parallel with pregnancy, while the normal human gestation period is nine *months.*

Studies of prehistoric art and religion suggest a widespread cult of the Great Goddess or Earth Mother that dates back to the Old Stone Age, some 30,000 years ago (see Gimbutas, 1989). In this cult women, fertility and maternity seem to have been the dominant themes, and it is possible that the social organization was matriarchal and matrilineal. With the emphasis being upon the 'female principle' it is also likely that the moon was a major cult object.

The cult of the Great Goddess appears to have persisted and dominated until comparatively recently in human history, perhaps until only some 5,000 years ago. Around this time, city states began to emerge, the wheel was invented, writing and mathematics first appeared, great astronomical advances were made, class systems were developed, and the whole of society became organized around a king at the centre, reflecting the new perceived order of the cosmos. Also at this time, religious functions began to be taken over by a male priesthood, patriarchy and patrilineal descent may have become more firmly established, and large-scale warfare was introduced into the human arena.

What we seem to be witnessing here is a takeover of society and religion by men. Although this change must have appeared gradual to those living through it, in the time scale of human evolution it was indeed sudden. With the rise of patriarchy, lunar cults of the Goddess were replaced by solar cults of the God-King. In these solar cults, the sun is generally male and is attributed with 'masculine' qualities such as strength, courage and fierceness. Associated with the hero, he is commonly depicted brandishing a sword or driving his golden horse-drawn chariot across the sky – all images of warfare and male bravado.

Although Goddess cults survived in many areas, they were generally driven underground or given minor importance within the new order. In ancient Egypt, for example, the earlier worship of the goddess Nuit (later Isis) was replaced by that of the sun-god Ra (later Osiris). In Greece also, worship of the most ancient goddess Gaia (the Earth Mother) was replaced by that of Zeus (the Sky Father). It is also revealing to note that Zeus became king of the gods by overcoming the Titans, themselves the children of Gaia.

Without doubt, male domination and the development of solar cults were accompanied by a certain degree of misogyny, suppression of women, and a general derogation of the 'female principle'. Women thus came to be considered feeble, anarchic, mad or evil, and their natural functions as unclean and taboo. Witches, for example, became traditionally female, while menstruation was thought of as an affliction or 'curse'. In many societies, menstruating women are placed apart from the community and are forbidden normal activities. The early Church Fathers even debated whether women had souls and many religions still consider women to be of inferior status.

THE HORIZONTAL DIMENSION: A SECOND LOOK

I have presented this brief historical survey in order to explain and clarify the meanings of right and left. If the theory of lunar and solar cults is correct, then right and left should be associated with male and female. Evidence for this is widespread. The Pythagorean Table of Opposites includes left with female and right with male. There is a theory, attributed to Anaxagoras, that girls are conceived from semen in the left testicle, boys from the right. At the turn of the present century the obstetrician E. Rumley Dawson (1909) put forward the equally extraordinary theory that boys come from ova that are fertilized in the right ovary, girls from the left ovary. According to tradition, Eve was formed from a rib on Adam's left side. Yogic philosophy teaches that a lunar (feminine) channel of energy (the *ida*) flows down the spine, starting from the left nostril; a solar (masculine) channel (the *pingala*) begins from the right nostril. In

Egyptian mythology the moon is believed to be the left eye of the High God, the sun is the right eye. In the Hebrew Cabala, the left pillar is female and is headed by *Binah* (the Great Sea); the right pillar is male, headed by *Chokmah* (the Supernal Father). Finally, at Christian weddings, the bride's family traditionally sits on the left, the bridegroom's on the right.

The evidence that an ancient lunar cult of the Great Goddess was suppressed in relatively modern times by male-oriented solar cults helps to place into context certain meanings generally attributed to the left and right. Thus, according to this interpretation, the *derogation* of the left and left-handedness (by association with weakness, falsity, impurity, abnormality, disorder, evil, taboo, etc.) may be a comparatively recent historical phenomenon. These associations may not, therefore, constitute the original or fundamental meaning of the left. Similarly, the original meaning of the right may not be based primarily on concepts such as strength, correctness, purity, normality, order, goodness or orthodoxy. These attributions may, in other words, simply reflect a male or patriarchal bias.

The primary distinction between left and right seems, therefore, not to be between good and bad (this distinction is, I believe, represented by the vertical polarity of up vs down). Rather it is between the moon-night-female principle on the left hand and the sun-day-male principle on the right. In order to understand fully the meanings of left and right it therefore becomes necessary to elaborate upon the major dichotomies that define or reflect these two principles. The most important polarities, based upon a variety of sources, are summarized in Table 3.

It should be noted that in including male and female in this table I am

Table 3 The symbolism of left and right

Left	Right	Left	Right
Moon	Sun	Instinct	Intellect
Night	Day	Maturation	Learning
Female	Male	Understanding	Knowledge
Dark	Light	Synthesis	Analysis
Negative	Positive	Pattern	Proposition
Passive	Active	Simultaneous	Sequential
Subjective	Objective	Love	Law
Changeable	Constant	Art	Science
Soft	Firm	Nonverbal	Verbal
Receptive	Creative	Music	Speech
Yin	Yang	Intuition	Logic
Mysterious	Manifest	Heart	Head
Fantasy	Reality	Emotion	Reason
Sleep	Wakefulness	Inner	Outer
Unconscious	Conscious	Introversion	Extraversion
Dream	Action	Covert	Overt

not suggesting for one moment that males necessarily show the characteristics on the right while females exhibit those on the left. It must be appreciated that the Goddess is a *symbol* for processes that involve the whole earth and all humanity – she is not a female *person*. The same may also be said of the 'male' sun-god. Night and day, moon and sun, female and male – every person has experienced these things and anyone who cares to look will find them at work within her or his own being. As well as indicating physical gender, the ideas of male and female may therefore also be understood as symbols of psychological polarities that exist within each individual, whether physically male or female. Psychologically, as the esoteric traditions teach, we are all androgynous.

The basis for gender symbolism rests, I believe, largely upon analogies that may be drawn between psychological attributes and the obvious and undeniable *physiological* differences between the sexes. These include, for example, differences in levels of subcutaneous fat (hence soft vs firm), differences between the form and function of the genitalia (e.g., mysterious vs manifest, inward vs outward) and differences in procreative roles (e.g., sustaining vs germinating). Introversion, for example, is therefore a psychological concept that may be *symbolized* by the female; extraversion by the male. But this does not mean that all females are introverted nor that males are extraverted. Neither does it imply that *on average* females are more introverted than males. We should always remember that we are talking about the male and female 'principles' – subtle complexes of meanings that may be usefully *symbolized* by physical gender – we are not referring to persons of each sex. In considering left–right symbolism it must also be realized that many polarities derive more directly from the principles of moon and sun, or night and day (e.g., dark vs light, dream vs action) rather than from female and male.

OUR TWO SIDES

Confirmation for many of the psychological polarities listed in Table 3 comes from evidence that they may in some way relate to the left and right sides of our bodies. It has been suggested, for example, that the way a person clasps the hands together reveals certain dominant characteristics. If the right thumb is on top, this is supposed to indicate reason and action, whereas if the left thumb is uppermost, then emotions, instincts, imagination and a generally passive nature are signified. In palmistry, the left hand traditionally expresses inborn characteristics, the right hand shows what we may become. One especially interesting theory is based upon the observation that the two sides of the human face are generally quite distinct in shape and expression (Wolff, 1933). The right face is supposed to show our conscious, everyday personality, while the left face reveals our darker, unconscious tendencies. Some support for this idea has come from recent experimental studies which show that the expression of positive emotion is mediated by the right face, negative emotion by the left (e.g., Schiff and MacDonald, 1990). Finally, the psychologist Robert Ornstein (1977) suggests that if we attempt to 'sense' each side of the body in turn, we will (at least if right-handed) probably feel our right side as being more masculine, light, active and logical; the left side as more feminine, dark, passive, intuitive, mysterious and artistic.

A possible explanation for these differences lies in the psychophysiology of the brain. It has been known for centuries that the brain or, more precisely, the *cerebral cortex* (the massive outer layer, responsible for thinking) is divided almost completely into two roughly symmetrical halves. These right and left *cerebral hemispheres* are connected by a large bundle of communicating fibres called the *corpus callosum*. Although the two hemispheres share many functions, each is also normally specialized for certain activities. These have been identified, for example, by observations of people who have suffered strokes or other damage in one hemisphere, as well as of so-called 'split-brain' patients whose corpus callosum has been surgically severed for medical reasons (see Bradshaw and Nettleton, 1981; Ornstein, 1973, 1977).

In discussing the cerebral hemispheres it must be appreciated that because of their *contralateral* connections to sensory and motor functions (for example, a stroke in the left hemisphere may cause paralysis and lack of sensation down the right side) our *experience* of the right is actually mediated in the first place by the *left* hemisphere; experience of the left is similarly mediated by the *right* hemisphere.

In right-handed people (the evidence from left-handers is less clear-cut) the left hemisphere (experienced as *right*) is usually specialized for speech and for verbal, mathematical, logical or analytical thinking. It is believed to process information in a linear, sequential fashion. Because of its verbal, rational functions, the left hemisphere has been compared with the conscious mind of psychoanalytic theory (Ornstein, 1977).

In contrast, the right hemisphere (experienced as *left*) is generally specialized for spatial orientation, non-verbal awareness, body image, pattern and face recognition, artistic and craft activities, musical appreciation, intuitive understanding and dreaming. It is believed to be capable of synthesizing, relating or integrating a variety of information which it processes simultaneously rather than sequentially. Because of its association with non-verbal awareness, intuition and dreaming, the right hemisphere has been compared with the psychoanalytic unconscious (ibid.).

For our purposes, the major import of this neuropsychological research lies in the powerful support it gives for the proposed meanings of left and right (it must always be remembered, of course, that in referring to the *left* we are actually implicating the right hemisphere, and vice versa). In demonstrating that many of the suggested psychological polarities relate clearly to the functioning of the brain, these studies indicate that we are talking about something quite fundamental to human experience. The

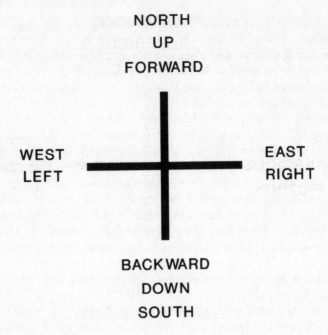

Figure 3 The Greek cross

symbolism of left and right, it seems, is based on more than idle super-
stition. Furthermore, because each person has two cerebral hemispheres,
this research serves to underline and develop the important point made
earlier that we all have the capacity to function in *both* ways.

THE SYMBOLISM OF THE CROSS

Having discussed the symbolic meanings of the vertical and horizontal
dimensions, we are now in a position to examine the way in which these
may be combined to provide a more complete understanding of an
individual's psychological situation.

The emblem of the cross predates its adoption by the Christian
community, having been used since prehistoric times. As a symbol, the
cross is not only complex, but also often highly charged with emotion. Its
specific meaning generally depends upon the particular form or shape that
the figure takes (compare, for example, the crucifix and the swastika). For
Christianity, the primary significance of the cross is as a reminder of the
Crucifixion, of Christ's suffering, and of His atonement for the sins of the
world. For other peoples, however, the cross may be a symbol of fire, the
sun or the life force (e.g., the Egyptian *ankh*).

In order to understand the Watchword matrix we need only consider the
simplest and earliest form of the cross. This is the equal-armed figure,

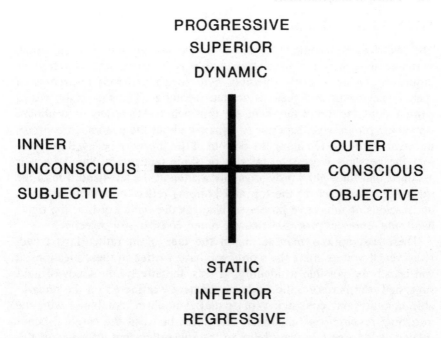

PROGRESSIVE
SUPERIOR
DYNAMIC

INNER   OUTER
UNCONSCIOUS   CONSCIOUS
SUBJECTIVE   OBJECTIVE

STATIC
INFERIOR
REGRESSIVE

Figure 4 The cross of self-realization

made from a single vertical and horizontal line, known as the Greek cross. The Greek cross is believed to represent the four directions as they radiate from a central point and thus to signify orientation in space (e.g., Cirlot, 1971). These directions may be variously interpreted as (a) north, south, west and east, or (b) up, down, left and right, or (c) forward, backward, left and right. In denoting the radiation of space from a single point, the Greek cross represents the centre of the cosmos. Since this cosmos may be interpreted not only physically but psychologically, the Greek cross also comes to symbolize the centre of consciousness and personal being.

The vertical line of the Greek cross, cut in two by the horizontal, signifies the division between the higher and lower worlds, between good and bad, between spirit and matter, between evolution and involution, or between future and past. Similarly, the horizontal line is divided into the left and right 'hands' of personal existence – unconscious and conscious, inner and outer, passive and active, feminine and masculine, or subjective and objective. Yet the cross is much more than a symbol of division. More fundamentally it carries the promise of balance, of union, of the conjunction of opposites. Psychologically therefore, as Carl Jung (e.g., 1968c, d) realized, the cross is a major symbol of self-realization or individuation (Figure 4).

THE WATCHWORD MATRIX

The Watchword technique is based on the assumption that the initial spontaneous generation of sixteen words is in some way coloured or influenced by an implicit (possibly neurologically based) awareness of spatial dimensions and their associated meanings. The first eight words, written along the top of the sheet, are thus believed to reflect or symbolize something progressive, superior or dynamic about the person. In contrast, the eight words written along the bottom of the sheet are believed to represent the person's regressive, inferior or static tendencies. Similarly, it is assumed that the eight words originally written at the left-hand side of the sheet (i.e., four each at the top and bottom) reflect or symbolize inner, unconscious or subjective processes, whereas the eight words at the right-hand side represent processes that are outer, conscious or objective.

These assumptions may seem, on the face of it, rather far-fetched. However, if you examine the words you have written in these locations, it will usually be possible to identify, at least tentatively, the kinds of links suggested. Furthermore, the evidence we have considered on the remarkable ubiquity and consistency of spatial symbolism, combined with the intriguing research on functional differences between the cerebral hemispheres, adds a certain plausibility to the suggestion that influence of this nature may somehow occur. The precise mechanism involved is, however, at present a complete mystery.

In order to reveal the psychological pattern more clearly, a series of connections is formed between pairs of words. This procedure enables the person to identify underlying themes and to uncover deeper layers of meaning. It may also be that this gives further opportunity for the words to be influenced by our awareness of spatial metaphor. At the same time, this progressive focusing tends to confound any conscious attempt to contrive responses. Certainly, as a result of this sequential process, many people find that although the initial set of sixteen words may seem trivial and psychologically unimportant, later connections are often strikingly significant.

When interpreting a Watchword matrix, only the eleven words within the inner rectangle are usually considered. Each of these is assigned a specific *key meaning* that derives from its location within the matrix. The Watchword keys are indicated in Figure 5.

In this matrix, *Giant* and *Dwarf* represent the vertical polarity of up vs down (progression vs regression). *Soul* and *Persona* represent the horizontal polarity of left vs right (inner vs outer).

The four corner keys indicate the various combinations of poles on these two main dimensions. Thus *Guide* is the principle of inner progression, *Imago* is outer progression, *Shadow* is inner regression, and *Spectre* is outer regression.

Station and *Battle* each represents a point of balance or tension between

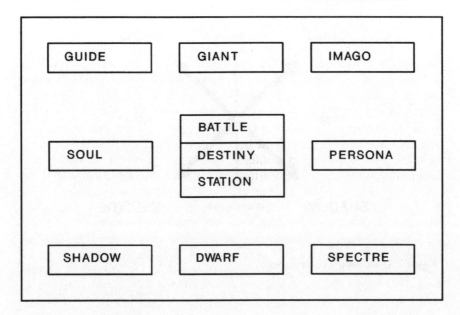

Figure 5 The Watchword keys

the two poles of, respectively, the inner–outer and progressive–regressive dimensions.

To complete the matrix, *Destiny* represents the final resolution of all forces, tensions and opposites within the psyche. Its immediate derivation, however, is from the union of *Station* and *Battle*.

These relationships are summarized in Figures 6–10, and in Table 4. Table 4 also includes the primary psychological indications of each key.

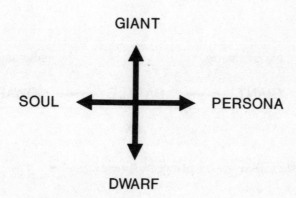

Figure 6 The principal dimensions

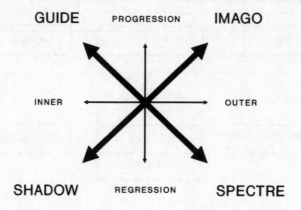

Figure 7 Dimensional combinations

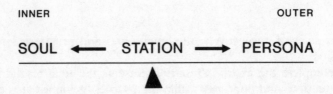

Figure 8 The balance/tension of inner and outer

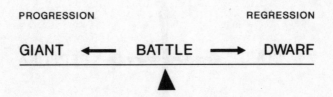

Figure 9 The balance/tension of progression and regression

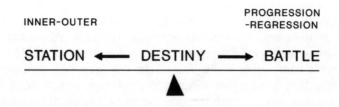

Figure 10 The final resolution

INSPECTING THE MATRIX

Before studying the detailed descriptions of each of the Watchword keys, provided in the next chapter, you might like to consider the extent to which the words you have written at each key location seem to reflect the ideas indicated in Table 4. The clearest relationships are often found with the four primary directions (*Giant, Dwarf, Soul, Persona*) and with the three central keys (*Station, Battle, Destiny*).

If there does not appear to be any obvious link between the words you have written in these locations and the corresponding key principles, it may be that you need to consider your words as symbols or metaphors. For example, *Giant* is often represented by words that symbolize *movement* (e.g., bus, train, road, swimming, flood, river). Such words may indicate some important change of direction in your life, or the need to be more dynamic in your general approach.

Table 4 Key principles and psychological indications

Key	Principle	Psychological indications
Giant	Progression	Driving forces
Dwarf	Regression	Inertial tendencies
Soul	Inwardness	Basic inner personality
Persona	Outwardness	Basic outer personality
Guide	Inner progression	Higher intuitions
Imago	Outer progression	Ego-ideals
Shadow	Inner regression	Repressed material
Spectre	Outer regression	Problems and anxieties
Station	Inner–outer balance or tension	Sense of basic selfhood
Battle	Progressive–regressive balance or tension	Personal task
Destiny	Final resolution	Realized self

Sometimes you will find that the word you have written appears to contradict the principle corresponding to a particular key. In most cases this seems to be only an apparent contradiction rather than a true reversal of polarity in the Watchword matrix. For this reason, you should always try to interpret your words in relation to the key meanings indicated before concluding that there is any reversal. For example, the word 'fail' in the *Giant* location may indicate that it is the fear of failure that is driving you forward. Again, the word 'clean' in the *Dwarf* location may suggest that an obsession with cleanliness is holding you back.

The question of whether there can be true reversals of polarity in the Watchword matrix (i.e., down for up, or right for left) is still unresolved. Over the years I have come across a number of cases in which a person has maintained that the polarity of one or both dimensions needed to be reversed in order to make sense of the matrix. In most of these cases, however, even though reversal is suggested at first sight, careful examination has revealed that a meaningful and helpful interpretation is possible on the basis of standard polarity.

One important complication that needs to be recognized is that ideas can sometimes represent their opposites. This is shown for example in irony, as well as in deliberate semantic inversions such as 'Little John' (meaning big) or the modern colloquial term 'wicked' (meaning excellent). In symbolism also, inversions of meaning are regularly found. Thus the fool or jester can represent wisdom, while death carries the promise of rebirth. It seems that all thought (thesis) contains the seeds of its own opposition (antithesis). As if to confirm this, I have known several cases where a person has crossed out a connecting word in the matrix only to write in its opposite. In practice this means that a word such as 'fail' in the *Giant* location might indicate that a major driving force is the desire for *success*. If this all sounds like a cop-out, then I am sorry. Unfortunately human thought is not as simple and unambiguous as we might like it to be. We must just accept, live with and finally learn from complexities of this kind.

Interestingly, apparent reversals seem to be more commonly claimed in relation to the left–right rather than the up–down dimension. This is due, I believe, more to the difficulty people have in distinguishing between what in their personality is truly 'inner' and what is 'outer' and does not reflect any genuine tendency towards reversal on this dimension. It should also be noted that, even though it might be suggested, on intuitive or theoretical grounds, that left–right polarity may vary according to handedness or gender, there are no clear indications of this. In contrast, like up and down, the left–right dimension appears to exhibit stable and universal significance.

The implication of this discussion is that you should almost always interpret your matrix on the basis of the standard polarity described in this book. It is most unlikely that reversing the matrix will improve matters in any way and, more importantly, allowing yourself to tinker with the system will only encourage you to find the interpretation that is most flattering or pleasing, rather than one that is accurate or helpful. In a real sense, the fixed structure of the Watchword matrix assumes the role of the 'other' in the essentially dialectical process of coming to know the self. The key meanings thus serve to confront and question your ideas about yourself in a way that may hopefully challenge you to achieve a new and greater understanding. True interrogation of the self is possible, however, only if the various keys are permitted to be themselves and are not rearranged at whim to suit our own self-images.

If you find it impossible to obtain a satisfactory interpretation in the standard fashion, then you *might* consider reversing the polarity of one or both dimensions (rewriting the matrix on a new form is the simplest method). For the reasons outlined above, this should not become a matter of routine, but should always be acknowledged to be a last, desperate measure. However, if reversal helps to establish a meaningful interpretation that was not possible before, then this procedure must be considered ultimately justified. After all, it is not good to be too dogmatic about these things.

4 The Watchword keys

ORGANIZATION

In this chapter, each of the Watchword keys is discussed in detail. The key descriptions are organized in the following sections:

Principle

Describes the dominant principles or fundamental ideas that are characteristic of the key. These principles derive directly from the organizational structure of the matrix.

General indications

Describes the major psychological forces, processes or tendencies that are indicated by the key.

Common themes

Lists the personal themes or areas of concern that are most commonly expressed in the key word.

Typical symbols

Lists a variety of metaphors, symbols and images that express important aspects of the key meaning. Many of these are often found at the corresponding key position within a Watchword matrix. In these cases it will be necessary during interpretation to decode their particular significance or message in the overall context of the matrix. Other 'traditional' symbols are also included in order to clarify and elaborate upon the associations involved.

It will be noticed that several symbols appear under more than one key. This is because most symbolic images are capable of expressing more than one idea. The sun may symbolize, for example, consciousness, or power, or success, or integration. When interpreting symbols it is helpful to bear in mind the principles that define the key under consideration. Thus, at *Giant*, the sun may represent power or drive, at *Persona* it may indicate extraversion or creativity, at *Imago* it may suggest status or success, and at *Destiny* it may symbolize completion or individuation. Although this may all seem frustratingly ambiguous to the logical mind, such complexities are an essential and inevitable feature of symbolic thought.

Comments

Discusses any important observations that have been made concerning the practical meaning and interpretation of the key. Included in this is a consideration of the major variations that are found in the way the key is expressed in the matrix. Parallels with Jungian concepts are also given where these apply.

LEARNING THE WATCHWORD KEYS

It is recommended that each key is studied carefully before you attempt seriously to interpret a Watchword matrix. While studying the various keys it can, however, be both interesting and informative to compare your own responses with the descriptions given.

It is not necessary to learn these key descriptions by heart. More important is the need to develop a good general understanding of, and 'feel' for, the meaning of each key. You should also pay particular attention to the interrelationships among keys. To this end, you will find it helpful to examine each key in terms of the basic structural principles of the Watchword matrix that are outlined in Chapter 3.

GIANT

Principle

Progression. Growth. Movement. Freedom. Maturity. Strength. Drive. Order. Forwardness. Future.

General indications

Driving forces. Dominant motivation. Source of strength. Creative impulses. Necessary movement or development. Features that are carrying the person forward. Future possibility. Personal virtues.

Common themes

Ambition. Fame. Success. Achievement. Money. Happiness. Change.

Movement. Freedom. Spontaneity. Playfulness. Travel. Will-power. Self-assertion. Work. Learning. Creativity. Clarity. Service. Self-sacrifice. Healing. Care. Religion. Hope. Love. Family. Friends. Relating. Procreation. Newness. Purity. Naturalness. Goodness. Order. Justice.

Typical symbols

White. Spring. Egg. Seed. Plant. Star. Space. Sky. Flight. Time. Spiral. Steps. Road. Mountain. Ship. Bus. Train. Car. Engine. Thighs. Thunderbolt. Oak. King. God. Jupiter. Zeus. Thor. Prince. Lord.

Comments

In essence, *Giant* tells us something about the person's fundamental motivation or orientation in life. Generally it indicates the major drives that are carrying the person forward. These are much more basic than the ego's conscious desires and goals (which are usually more clearly reflected in *Imago*).

For many people, the main emphasis is upon personal success, achievement and happiness although, for some, the orientation is towards service, caring and self-sacrifice. Other important life-positions indicated by *Giant* may emphasize intellectual, political, artistic or family ideals.

Giant can also refer to virtuous, progressive or creative qualities in the self or in one's current situation. Alternatively, it may simply point to the need for change and growth, or to the importance of being more dynamic in one's approach to life.

DWARF

Principle

Regression. Decay. Stagnation. Inhibition. Immaturity. Weakness. Apathy. Chaos. Backwardness. Past.

General indications

Inertial tendencies. Source of weakness. Features that are holding the person back. Characteristics that should be held in check or moderated. Earlier situation. Childhood. Immature impulses. Personal vices.

Common themes

Negativity. Despair. Depression. Tiredness. Boredom. Stagnation. Laziness. Failure. Claustrophobia. Restriction. Frigidity. Impotence.

Confusion. Folly. Madness. Anxiety. Carelessness. Clumsiness. Falsity. Sin. Evil. Dirt. Decay. Grief. Death. Coldness. Sickness. Violence. Conflict. Disunion. Criticism. Examinations. Cynicism. Materialism. Cheapness. Habit. Social pressure. Cautiousness. Immaturity. Infancy. Childishness. Stuffiness. Old-fashioned.

Typical symbols

Black. Winter. Ice. Death. Tomb. Worm. Skeleton. Mud. Scythe. Saturn. Devil. Underworld. Abyss. Waste Land. Emptiness. Ruins. Chaos. Madman. Broken sword. War. Blood. Knife. Red. Chains. Prison. Snail. Bed. Victorian. Antique. Baby. Toys. Lead. Tin.

Comments

Dwarf generally indicates either (a) the past, or the direction from which the person has come, (b) problems or difficulties that are preventing forward movement or (c) personal inadequacies and weaknesses. Themes that are frequently associated with *Dwarf* centre around problems of personal apathy and inertia, immaturity, social restriction, depression, anxiety and stress.

While *Dwarf* is basically a negative force, there is almost always a positive lesson to be learnt from this key. Thus, for example, as it makes us aware of what is holding us back, or of major weaknesses in our character, we may take steps to counteract these negative influences. It is important to realize that there is nothing fixed, immutable or inevitable about any part of the Watchword matrix. *Dwarf* does not, therefore, represent a permanent fault or insurmountable problem, but rather it shows us those features of our character or situation that need to be overcome or worked upon in a constructive fashion.

SOUL

Principle

Inwardness. Subjectivity. Unconsciousness. Containment. Receptivity. Passivity. Mystery.

General indications

Basic inner personality. Private or subjective self. Thoughts and feelings. Emotional situation. Unconscious or concealed tendencies. Attitude to the unconscious. Qualities that we are attracted to (or are frightened of) in the opposite sex. Jungian *anima* or *animus*.

Common themes

Emotions. Affections. Memories. Feelings of contentment or discontent. Security or insecurity. Innocence. Sweetness. Gentleness. Cultural roots. Close family. Cosiness. Togetherness. Romance. Love. Laughter. Childhood. Schooldays. Listening. Concealment. Darkness. Mystery. Strangeness. Contradiction. Disguise. Depth. Heaviness. Flexibility. Uniqueness. Autonomy. Decision.

Typical symbols

Forest. Cloak. Curtain. Green. Moon. Night. Closet. Shed. Pot. Urn. Cavern. Well. Water. Sea. Whirlpool. Pet. Cherub. Rose. Lips. Sleeping Beauty. Home. Door. Key. Wedding. Slippers. Narcissus. Mirror. Brain. Plastic. Clown.

Comments

Soul essentially represents some aspect of the person's 'inner workings'. At times the word written at this location may simply reflect a dominant thought, memory or feeling, usually one that is kept private or secret or one that is largely unconscious. At other times, *Soul* can suggest something of the fundamental style or nature of the person's intimate, subjective self. This is the self that generally is known only to the self and perhaps to a few close friends; the self that we often refer to as the 'real me' or 'inner me'.

For some people the inner self can be a mysterious, unmapped territory, one that they may be fascinated by but are perhaps unwilling to explore. Such a possibility is often suggested when words in this location indicate strangeness, depth or darkness.

Soul can also represent personal qualities or characteristics to which we are strongly attracted but that we fail to recognize as part of our own nature. Instead, we often look for these qualities in other people, generally members of the opposite sex. In the terminology of Jungian analytical psychology, this aspect of *Soul* is referred to as a contrasexual *soul image* – in males a female *anima*, in females a male *animus* (see, for example, Jacobi, 1968; Jung, 1966, 1968a, b). Thus, for example, men are often attracted to women they perceive to be gentle, caring or motherly, whereas women may be attracted to men they see as dominant, assertive or self-confident. Jung believed that only by recognizing and accepting the qualities we find attractive in the opposite sex as important components of our own psyche could we become fully-rounded human beings.

Alternatively the soul image may, especially when contaminated with elements of the Jungian *shadow* (to be considered later), express itself in a negative way, perhaps revealed by objectionable characteristics that a person attributes to (projects upon) members of the opposite sex. Thus a man may see women as vain, bitchy or moody, while a woman may criticize men for being domineering, insensitive or brutal. Because this projection is essentially of the person's own repressed (unconscious) qualities, the negative soul image can often erupt into consciousness in times of stress or difficulty. In this way, the man may himself become vain, bitchy or moody, while the woman may act in a domineering, insensitive or brutal fashion. Once again, the important task for the person is to become aware of these unconscious tendencies, to accept them as important facets of his or her own personality, and ultimately to integrate them meaningfully into the total pattern of the psyche.

PERSONA

Principle

Outwardness. Objectivity. Consciousness. Expansiveness. Creativity. Activity. Openness. Communication.

General indications

Basic outer personality. Public or objective self. Mask or performances. Social roles. Physical or social situation. Conscious attitudes and tendencies. Jungian *persona*.

Common themes

Public or social life. Career. Social status. Self-presentation. Advertising. Personal efficiency or inefficiency. Adequacy or inadequacy. Performance. Public assessment of self. Physical appearance. Body image. Sexuality. Leisure. Holidays. Exercise. Sport. Activity. Fun. Fortune. Spontaneity. Creativity. Self-disclosure. Openness. Communication. Speech. Writing. Display. Outer expression of emotions. Noise. Spectacle. Firmness. Falseness. Insincerity. Coldness. Meaninglessness. Escape.

Typical symbols

City. Arena. Public place. Air. Street. Garden. Hotel. Theatre. Mask. Face. Eye. Legs. Mouth. Smoking. Sun. Suntan. Torch. Fire. Flying. Wings. Logos. Book. Magazine. Letters. Pen. Explosion. Bang. Machine. Ice. Puppet.

Comments

Persona, equivalent to Jung's concept of the same name, represents some aspect of the person's 'outer workings' (see, for example, Jacobi, 1968;

Jung, 1966, 1971). Often the word in this location indicates a dominant current interest or activity, usually one that is publicly exhibited or that involves other people. This may focus upon career, social life, sport or other leisure activity.

More generally, *Persona* represents the self that is known to others, the self that we offer as an object for public display and assessment. This public self is primarily physical (hence the commonly expressed concern with appearance and sexual attractiveness). It is also the means by which we interact with and influence other people, both verbally and non-verbally. For this reason, *Persona* often reflects themes of interpersonal communication.

The typical *style* of behaviour expressed by the public self is what we ordinarily mean by 'personality'. For example a person may be described as 'friendly', or 'nervous', or 'impatient', because that is how they generally come across to others. *Persona* can often indicate the more dominant features of this outer personality. Alternatively, because the public self also exists as an object in the social world, *Persona* sometimes reflects social roles or the individual's position within a social network.

For many people, the public self represents the most important area of their life. Such people have often mistakenly *identified* with their outer personality, and their major concern is usually to maintain and enhance their attractiveness or status in the eyes of others. This approach to life is particularly hazardous, not only because it neglects the equally important subjective side of our nature, but also because it makes us totally dependent upon achieving acceptance and approval from other people. We therefore constantly seek attention in order to confirm the sense of our own existence. At the same time we are always aware of the possibility of losing the favour of others. This in turn may lead to continual anxiety about our desirability, adequacy, efficiency or social acceptability.

For other people, the outer personality may seem to be a false and insincere mask or set of performances, behind which the 'real self' is concealed. It is interesting to note in this context that the English words 'person' and 'personality' (and *Persona*) derive from the Latin *persona*, referring to the mask traditionally worn by characters in a drama. This attitude to the outer personality or public self is often revealed in the Watchword matrix when the word at this location suggests falseness, suspicion, coldness or meaninglessness.

At its most positive, *Persona* can indicate a spirit of openness, candour, spontaneity and creative activity. In such cases the public self seems not to be viewed as masking or concealing the person's 'true' inner nature, but is perhaps understood as the means of outer expression for private thoughts, emotions and creative impulses.

GUIDE

Principle

Inner progression. Spirituality. Higher sensitivity. Light. Inspiration. Subjective good.

General indications

Higher self. Sense of inner teacher. Inner power or greatness. Intuitive insights. Dominant sense modality. Main source of inspiration or enjoyment. Inner qualities that need to be fully acknowledged or developed. Conscience. Moral principles. Ideology. Message from the unconscious. The direction of unconscious striving. Jungian *mana personality*.

Common themes

Wisdom. Education. Culture. Humanity. Being. Order. Law. Conscience. Guilt. Ideology. Leader. Nature. Creation. Caring. Love. Richness. Spirituality. Intuition. Message. Senses. Relaxation. Comfort. Peace. Warmth. Happiness. Vitality. Adventure. Celebration. Unknown. Potential. Forbiddance. Need. Development.

Typical symbols

Animal. Fur. Bird. Dove. Owl. Feather. Wings. Bee. Butterfly. Angel. Fairy. Sky. Blue. Sun. Star. Nose. Smell. Food. Honey. Attic. Vault. Anchor. Countryside. Garden. Child. Picnic. Dance. Circus. Wise man. Shaman. Priest. Sage. Prophet. Wise woman. Earth Mother. Magna Mater. Sybil. Priestess. Doctor. Professor. Hermit. Scribe. Church. Temple. Christ. Buddha. Krishna. Whisper. Bell. Book. Candle. Lamp. Lantern.

Comments

Guide generally indicates the 'higher' or 'better' side of our inner nature, or something that is essential for our inner growth or happiness. For many people, this is represented by education, religion, nature, art, morality or social-political activity. For others, however, the dominant concern seems to be with the achievement of sensory pleasure or feelings of personal contentment.

It is not too far amiss to suggest that *Guide* represents our personal idea of God, of goodness, or of ultimate happiness. Certainly the word written at this location often seems to express or symbolize the person's deepest inner yearnings or sense of personal rightness, although at other times *Guide* may simply reflect a passing whim or temporary insight. No matter how trivial it may seem, however, this is a key that should always be given careful consideration for it often carries an important message about the direction in which we need to move for inner growth.

The important thing to realize about *Guide* is that it usually reflects a subtle, seemingly inevitable and often unconscious striving. The goal or 'god' towards which this key indicates we are drawn is not primarily of our own choosing, nor something that we have been taught to value (cf. *Imago*). Instead it seems to be an ideal that we naturally favour. In practice, this ideal may or may not be in tune with our consciously expressed values.

Guide overlaps considerably with Jung's concept of the *mana personality* (see, for example, Jacobi, 1968; Jung, 1966). '*Mana*' is a Polynesian word referring to the elemental forces of nature, and the mana personality is basically the fountainhead of the person's sense of her or his innermost power, greatness, fascination or charisma. Jung saw the mana personality also as the primary root source of our essential maleness or femaleness. For this reason, Jung argued that the mana personalities of men and women differ fundamentally in nature and function.

The male mana personality is symbolized by the archetype of the *Wise Old Man*, the personification of spirit or, perhaps more accurately, of materialized spirit (Jacobi, 1968). The male principle therefore represents the bringing down to earth of 'higher' spiritual power. The female mana personality, on the other hand, is symbolized by the archetype of the *Great Earth Mother* (Magna Mater). This is the personification of matter or, more accurately, of spiritualized matter (ibid.). Thus the female principle represents the idea that matter itself (Nature *her*self) is suffused with spirit. These differences between the 'principles' of each sex may help to explain why, for example, natural magic is generally considered a female pursuit, whereas theurgy is traditionally male. The archetypes are also, I believe, related historically to the cults of the Great Goddess and the Sun-King or Sky Father discussed in Chapter 3.

Like the anima and animus, the mana personalities may in practice manifest both positively and negatively. In their positive forms, these archetypes are revealed in spirituality, wisdom, inner strength and love. In their negative expressions they can lead to arrogance, self-glorification and overweening pride. These negative manifestations are particularly likely when the person fails consciously to *differentiate* the mana personality as a partial aspect of the total personality, but instead becomes overwhelmed by or identifies with this archetype. This, Jung believed, was the road to megalomania.

IMAGO

Principle

Outer progression. Material success. Achievement. Physical and social development. Objective good.

General indications

Ego-ideals. Conscious values, goals and desires. Idealized image of the self. Imagined future situation or seemingly inevitable consequence of current trends. Physical, material or social need.

Common themes

Money. Possessions. Greed. Pleasure. Excitement. Satisfaction. Fame. Achievement. Career. Art. Compulsion. Obsession. Dream. Vision. Goals. Connection. Relationship. Sexual experience. Marriage. Family. Effort. Energy. Power. Control. Rulership. Clarity. Intelligence. Wandering. Confusion. Collapse. Suffering. Death.

Typical symbols

Shops. Bank. Cake. Ice-cream. Jewellery. Ring. Summer. Sun. Flowers. Flag. Victory. Medal. Crown. Eagle. Helmet. Crest. King. Statue. Fool. Arrow. Hero. Trumpet. Car. Running. River. Hills. Glass. Polishing.

Comments

Imago usually represents the conscious goals that we have for the (objective) self. Typically these are things that we have learned to value and desire. The themes most frequently expressed in this key centre around (a) material success, (b) physical enjoyment, (c) status and power and (d) romance and marriage. At other times, however, *Imago* can indicate an end that we do not seek but that may seem to be inevitable (e.g., illness, death, failure).

Occasionally the key does not directly reveal the end towards which we consciously strive, or seem to be drawn, but rather points to something that we must carry out or overcome in order to achieve more ultimate goals. This may take the form of suggesting the manner or style of behaviour that we must adopt in order to progress further in our public life, career or social relationships.

More fundamentally, *Imago* reflects an idealized image of the future self. This idealized self-image reveals our fantasy of the person that we believe we must become in order to gain maximum attention or acceptance from other people.

Many psychologists, existential philosophers and religious thinkers have pointed to the dangers of accepting and following this idealized fantasy of the self. Most importantly, because the idealized self is believed to be the outcome of other people's opinions of and desires for the self (e.g., those of our parents, teachers or friends) it does not necessarily reflect the person's 'natural' or 'real' needs and talents. For this reason it is often considered to represent false, inauthentic ideals that we would do better to ignore altogether. Instead, it is often argued, we should look inward to our own subjective experience in order to discover the 'true' direction our life should take (cf. Daniels, 1988).

In the context of the present model, however, the major problem that may be identified is the possibility of exclusive concern with the outer, objective side of one's being, at the expense of inner, subjective development. *Imago* is an important *part* of the psyche and we should become aware of its influence and role in our total make-up. It should not be allowed to dominate our existence, but then neither should any other aspect (and this includes inner, subjective experience).

SHADOW

Principle

Inner regression. Darkness. Denial. Repression. Subjective evil.

General indications

Repressed material. Dark or hidden side of person's nature. Disliked characteristics that the person is unwilling to recognize in the self and tends to project onto others. Qualities, functions or attitudes that the person has failed consciously to differentiate or develop. Irrational sensitivities. Complexes. Feelings of disgust. Inner weakness. Jungian *shadow*.

Common themes

Sex. Dirt. Pain (or pleasure). Unhappiness (or happiness). Tears (or laughter). Unattractiveness (or attractiveness). Hate. Prejudice. Violence. Cowardice. Oppression. Illness. Addiction. Death. Dreaminess. Disappointment. Emptiness. Weakness. Laziness. Loneliness. Waiting. Stasis. Strangeness. Confusion. Curiosity. Judgement.

Typical symbols

Sunset. Moon. Night. Sleep. Ocean. Forest. Invisibility. Cauldron. Cave. Devil. Leviathan. He-goat. Neptune. Hecate. Witch. Serpent. Dragon. Funeral. Church. Tar. Pollution. Litter. Soil. Touch. Body. Clothes. Robbery. Guns. Knife. Dagger. Hanging. Winter. Death.

Comments

Shadow in the Watchword matrix is essentially identical with Carl Jung's archetype of the same name (see, for example, Jacobi, 1968; Jung 1968a, b). *Shadow* represents our dark, hidden, repressed nature. It is the side of our character that we reject or deny because it conflicts with our conscious tendencies or our opinions about the self. Often we *project* our shadow onto other people and see in them the qualities that we fail to recognize in ourselves. For this reason, whenever we show a strong irrational tendency to criticize or blame others, we should consider whether in fact the fault we are condemning is really our own.

It is important to realize that *Shadow* does not always express negative, inferior or evil qualities in the self. Although violence, hatred, laziness, prejudice, cowardice, and slovenliness are themes that are commonly found, it may also be that positive qualities are being repressed. Many people, for example, are unwilling to recognize their own potential for inner happiness, vitality, creativity, empathy, altruism or intelligence. For these individuals it is always other people who possess such qualities.

No matter whether our shadow seems positive or negative, it is important to become aware of this side of our nature, not only so that we can accept (and therefore begin to moderate) our own failings, but also so that we can relate to other people in a genuine, open and uncontaminated fashion, without projecting onto them quite false or inappropriate characteristics.

SPECTRE

Principle

Outer regression. Material difficulty or failure. Physical and social degeneration. Objective evil.

General indications

Problems of living. Anxieties and fears. Areas where expression is difficult. Rejected values. Old preoccupations. Features a person is aware of in the self or situation but fundamentally dislikes. Dread of becoming. Area where help is needed or sought. Escapist tendencies. Domineering force.

Common themes

Failure. Problems. Examinations. Frustration. Inadequacy. Exhaustion. Uncertainty. Unhappiness. Insults. Anxiety. Dirt. Sexuality. Nakedness. Illness. Danger. Death. Chaos. Addiction. Drunkenness. Madness. Violence. Destruction. Meaninglessness. Freedom. Escape. Communication.

Typical symbols

Knife. War. Blood. Funeral. Rain. Stew. Stain. Soap. Bandage. Knot. Crash. Tunnel. Black. Devil. Rat. Dog. Ogre. Beast. Monster. Monkey. Locusts. Hog. Pig. Fox. Ass. Clown. Puppet. Infant. Drink. Drugs.

Comments

In essence, *Spectre* represents any feature of our personality or situation that is preventing us from adapting to or achieving success in the social or material world. Commonly expressed sources of difficulty are (a) problems with relationships, family, career, finance, etc., (b) crippling anxieties, fears or phobias, (c) a preoccupation with the past or with maintaining the status quo, (d) a tendency towards escapism or the avoidance of problems, (e) illness or exhaustion, (f) fear of freedom or of responsibility, (g) a failure of will or lack of courage.

At first glance, *Spectre* may seem to share much in common with *Dwarf*. The major distinction is that *Dwarf* tends to indicate very basic weaknesses, problems or difficulties that can dominate one's whole character and behaviour. *Spectre*, on the other hand, is much more situational and specific. It generally refers to particular (and often temporary) difficulties that relate clearly to one's lack of social or material success.

In addition to indicating sources of difficulty, *Spectre* sometimes directly reflects our major conscious fears and anxieties. *Spectre* can thus encapsulate those qualities or characteristics that consciously we most abhor or that we dread becoming. Similarly, *Spectre* may indicate values that we strongly reject, perhaps those that we associate with our parents or with our past. It should be noted in this context that *Spectre* represents a conscious (usually rational) rejection of unpleasant characteristics, distinguishing it from *Shadow* which generally signifies unconscious denial, repression or projection.

STATION

Principle

Inner–outer balance or tension. Point of contact between private and public lives. Basic form or style of being.

General indications

Sense of self. Current status or essential personal situation. Basic quality in the person. Continuing preoccupation. General emotional tone. Personal style. Identity problems. Jungian *ego*.

Common themes

Places. Persons. Objects. Shapes. Occupations. Activities. Beliefs. Memories. Emotions. Time. Security or insecurity. Uncertainty. Difficulty. Tension.

Typical symbols

Man. Animal. Hermaphrodite. Marriage. Mind. Head. Place. Cell. Home. Hearth. House. Bath. Window. Door. Stone. Statue. Town. City. Island. Diary. Name. Now. Me. Clothes. Mirror. Wax. Bowl. Urn. Threshold. Bridge. Ford. Guardian. Labyrinth.

Comments

Station is the most individual and idiosyncratic of the Watchword keys. As a result, the words written in this location tend to be rather more diverse than those at other key positions. These words seem essentially to reflect the person's sense of his or her own uniqueness, and often have a cryptic or very private significance that cannot be understood by another. At other times the word may capture the individual's 'essence' so effectively that it may almost be considered a kind of personal motto. Sometimes animal names or themes may be used as symbols of the person's basic style.

Conceptually, *Station* represents the union of the individual's private and public existence, or of the inner and outer personalities. It is the centre of our conscious being, experienced as the sense of basic identity and personal continuity. In this respect it is more or less identical with Jung's concept of the *ego* (see, for example, Jacobi, 1968; Jung, 1968b, 1969, 1971).

In practice, the word written at this location usually indicates something that is particularly important to the sense of self. Often this takes the form of (a) a dominant personal characteristic, interest or activity, (b) a basic life-role (e.g., mother, doctor, priest), (c) physical appearance, (d) the family, nation or ethnic group, (e) a major life experience, (f) a hero or idol, (g) the home or personal possessions or (h) a fundamental belief or attitude.

Many people, particularly the young, may not yet have achieved a clear sense of identity. Many others, especially at times of personal trauma or major life changes, may find their sense of identity under threat. Identity problems and personal crises are often indicated by words in the *Station* location that suggest uncertainty, insecurity, difficulty or tension.

BATTLE

Principle

Progressive–regressive balance or tension. Quest. Mission. Fight. Moral conflict.

General indications

Personal task, quest or adventure. Field of conflict. Moral dilemma. Inner turmoil. Spiritual crisis. Major cause of concern. Way forward.

Common themes

Conflict. Chaos. Anarchy. Order. Bondage. Oppression. Freedom. Revolution. Crisis. Opposites. Strength. Courage. Reliability. Morality. Learning. Intelligence. Religion. Transcendence. Humanity. Caring. Productivity. Change. Birth. Help. Truth vs falsity. Safety vs growth. Maturity vs immaturity.

Typical symbols

Cross. Mutiny. Battle. War. Hercules. Minotaur. Youth. Hero. Chariot. Sword. Teeth. Trap. Boxing. Playground. Tie. Chain. Catch. Ruin. Spike. Jazz. Church. Fall. Rising. Journey. Path. Pilgrim. Slippery.

Comments

Battle is a particularly important key that represents a major choice that the self must make. This choice is essentially between growth and safety, between moving forward and moving back (or between moving and remaining stationary). Often this is expressed in moral terms as a choice between good and evil, right and wrong, order and chaos, or truth and falsity.

Battle is a symbol of the *self in motion*, in contrast with *Station* which represents the static self. *Battle* points to the fact that there is always a task that we must fulfil, a meaning or purpose that must be realized, a goal or ideal that we should attempt to achieve. In practice, the word written in this location tends to indicate either (a) an area of one's life where choice, decision or action is necessary, (b) the importance of being more decisive, active or courageous in one's general approach, (c) a way forward that should be followed in order to realize one's basic purpose or (d) the possibility of spiritual or moral failure.

Although, on occasions, *Battle* may apparently refer to minor problems and conflicts, these should always be looked at more deeply to see whether something fundamental might lie beneath them. *Battle* is a central key in the Watchword matrix and it should never be dismissed lightly. What seems at first sight a trivial concern can often mask, reflect or symbolize a basic moral conflict or spiritual crisis.

DESTINY

Principle

Final resolution. Ending. Victory. Regeneration. Transformation.

General indications

Realized self. Projected outcome of battle or quest. Ultimate goal or value. Personal transformation. Jungian *self*.

Common themes

Time. Wholeness. Completion. Fulfilment. Contentment. Health. Love. Peace. Silence. Beauty. Justice. Truth. Faith. Salvation. Achievement. Control. Power. Success. Career. Money. Reward. Richness. Perseverance. Life. Rebirth. Regeneration. Family. Parenthood. Divorce.

Typical symbols

Snow. Heaven. Government. Throne. King. Sun. Lion. Cub. Smoke. Compost. Greenhouse. Storm. Fire. Explosion. Bomb. Ferry. Stop. Shake. Medal. Treasure. Jewel. Rose. Pearl. Prize. Ring. Circle. Grail.

Comments

Destiny is the central focus and final culmination of the Watchword matrix, having been derived as a result of combining all keys and balancing all polarities. Conceptually, therefore, *Destiny* is equivalent to Jung's concept of the realized *self*, the theoretical midpoint of the psyche achieved when all psychological opposites and contradictions have been harmoniously balanced and integrated (see, for example, Jacobi, 1968; Jung, 1968b, c).

In general terms, *Destiny* indicates the projected outcome of the self's journey through life, its anticipated final state or resting place. More than any other key, *Destiny* reveals our most basic values and goals, encapsulated in our personal understanding of self-perfection or self-realization.

Destiny often reflects the so-called 'eternal verities' (e.g., wholeness, love, peace, beauty, honour, justice, order, truth, faith) although other frequently expressed values focus upon more worldly concerns such as success, control or power. Sometimes *Destiny* does not itself directly indicate an ultimate goal or value but rather points to the necessity of a fundamental transformation or regeneration in one's situation or personality.

When interpreting *Destiny*, it should be remembered that Watchword is a system of psychological analysis and not a method of fortune telling. This key does not, therefore, indicate something that is destined to happen. *Destiny* essentially represents our current beliefs concerning the fundamental purpose or goal of our life and, like the other Watchword keys, its meaning must be sought in terms of our present psychological make-up. *Destiny* can suggest something that we think may happen, but not something that definitely will.

Furthermore, the key should always be interpreted psychologically (or spiritually) rather than physically. If *Destiny* seems to refer to a particular material outcome, this is usually a symbol or metaphor for an underlying psycho-spiritual process. Thus if the word you have written in this location is 'crash', this does not mean that you will shortly have a road accident. It might indicate, however, that some kind of personal crisis or failure is anticipated. More importantly, if (as is fairly common) the word signifies death, this is not a curse or omen. Instead it probably points either to the individual's basic pessimism or else to the need for a fundamental transformation in attitudes or circumstances.

5 Psychological types

When the matrices of several individuals are compared, the most obvious differences between them are usually in the *types* of words written at the key locations. In contrast, differences in the original sixteen words are generally much less apparent. It seems, therefore, that a major factor distinguishing matrices is the cognitive strategy or underlying thought processes used to derive associations. For example, some people form concrete associations, based upon objective, physical or perceptual links between images. A second group forms abstract, conceptual or analytic connections. Yet others seem to base their associations upon subjective, emotional or affective considerations. Finally, there is a group of people whose linking words may variously appear purposeful, imaginative, arbitrary or deep.

These differences in strategy seem to reflect more or less exactly Carl Jung's understanding of the four *functions of consciousness.* If this is the case, it raises the important possibility that the Watchword matrix may provide a way of assigning individuals to the *Jungian types.* Before we consider how this may be done in practice, it will be necessary to review briefly Jung's (e.g., 1971) theory of psychological types.

THE FUNCTIONS OF CONSCIOUSNESS

Jung suggests that there are four ways in which the conscious mind may apprehend reality, i.e., sensation, intuition, thinking and feeling. According to Jung, these four functions are arranged in two pairs of opposites. Firstly there are the *irrational* (or, better, non-rational) or perceiving functions of sensation and intuition. Secondly there are the *rational* or judging functions of thinking and feeling.

The non-rational functions

Sensation refers to our immediate experience of the objective world, a process that takes place without any kind of evaluation of the experience. Sensation perceives objects as they are – realistically and concretely. It fails to consider context, implications, meanings or alternative interpretations, but instead attempts to represent factually and in detail the information that is available to the senses.

Intuition refers to a deeper perception of inherent possibilities and inner meanings. Intuitive perception ignores the details and focuses instead upon the general context or atmosphere. It perceives (without clear evidence or proof) the direction in which things are moving, the subtle inner relationships and underlying processes involved, or the latent potentialities of a situation. Intuition never directly reflects reality but actively, creatively, insightfully and imaginatively adds meaning by reading things into the situation that are not immediately apparent to a purely objective observer.

The rational functions

Thinking is a mode of evaluation that is concerned with the truth or falsity of experience. It is based upon the intellectual comprehension of things and, in particular, of their conceptual interrelationships. It is a rational, systematic process that seeks to understand reality through analysis and logical inference.

Feeling is an affective, sentimental function. It involves judging the value of things or having an opinion about them on the basis of our likes and dislikes. Experiences are therefore evaluated in terms of good and bad, pleasant or unpleasant, acceptable or unacceptable. Feeling is not quite the same as emotion because we can like or dislike something, or express sentimental attachments without becoming emotional. Emotion is, however, one important manifestation of the feeling function.

Functional relationships

Although every person potentially exhibits all four functions, Jung believed that for most people one function will be dominant or superior, depending largely upon innate, constitutional factors. Whatever function is uppermost, the opposite (inferior) function will generally be unavailable to consciousness but instead, through the *principle of compensation*, will characterize the functioning of the unconscious. In practice this means that the inferior function will generally be repressed, or expressed in primitive, archaic, infantile and uncoordinated ways. For example, a person whose conscious mind functions in a thinking mode will usually have difficulty in expressing feelings and emotions. When feelings are expressed, these will typically take the form of infantile fantasies or eruptions of instinctual emotion. Conversely, a person with a superior feeling function will generally have difficulty in thinking systematically or logically. Attempts at conceptual thought in such people will often appear childish and banal.

In the same way, sensation and intuition are functional opposites because it is impossible simultaneously to perceive both the surface and

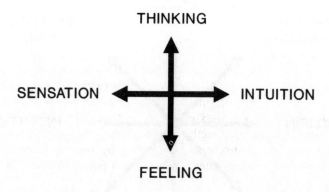

Figure 11 The functions of consciousness

beneath the surface of reality. If sensation is the dominant function, there will usually be a failure of imagination, vision or insight. When intuition is expressed this will tend to be unconscious, primitive and uncoordinated as, for example, in superstitious beliefs or unfounded jealousies. In contrast, an intuitive person often has difficulty in coming to terms with concrete reality or may express sensation in puerile ways such as food fads or through hypochondriacal tendencies.

In addition to the dominant function, most people have some conscious access to one function from the other pair of opposites. Thus a thinking person may have sensation or intuition as an *auxiliary function*, while an intuitive person may exhibit some thinking or feeling. Jung believed that few people are able to utilize both members of the other pair, even though the opposition between these is less than that between the superior and inferior functions. In theory, the process of personality development makes it possible to raise all four functions into consciousness. In practice, however, such psychological completeness is both difficult and rare.

An example of these functional relationships is illustrated in Figure 11. In placing thinking at the top, the diagram implies that thinking is the dominant function for this person, whereas feeling is inferior. The two other functions (i.e., sensation and intuition) are potential auxiliaries. The diagram does not, however, imply a left–right distinction between the auxiliary functions.

The function types

Jung's theory implies that eight basic *function types* are possible. These comprise the four single functions, together with the four possible

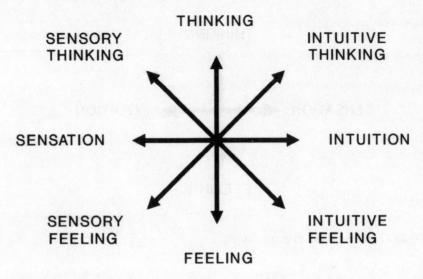

Figure 12 The eight function types

combinations of superior and auxiliary functions (which are not differentiated for this purpose). These eight types are illustrated in Figure 12.

THE ATTITUDES OF CONSCIOUSNESS

In addition to the four functions of consciousness, Jung recognized two basic *attitudes* that consciousness may take, which he calls *introversion* and *extraversion*. These attitudes are supposedly based upon the two directions in which a person's interests and energies may flow – either inward to subjective experience and psychological processes, or outward to the environment of objects, other people and collective norms. Jung believed that our characteristic attitude is basically inborn but that it can be changed, for example through psychoanalysis.

The terms 'introversion' and 'extraversion' are now common currency, both among psychologists and laypeople. Unfortunately the meanings of these terms have often been altered subtly from Jung's original understanding, generally towards considering them as different ways of *behaving* in social situations. In Jung's theory, however, introversion and extraversion represent two fundamental attitudes of *consciousness* rather than distinct types of social behaviour. Although behaviour normally reflects conscious attitudes, in certain cases it may be dominated by unconscious (opposite and compensatory) tendencies.

The attitude types

According to Jung, introverts (those whose conscious attitude is introverted) desire to become abstracted from the external environment. In seeking to conserve their energies within the self, they hesitate from investing interest in the outside world and may recoil from objects and people. This means that they are always rather defensive. Typically, introverts are reserved, shy, rather impenetrable individuals who are often poorly adjusted to their social environment. On the other hand, they are generally well adjusted to their inner world and, being introspective by nature, usually have clear subjective views and preferences.

In direct contrast, extraverts (those who are consciously extraverted) are fascinated by everything in the external world – objects, people, events and collective ideas. Moreover everything they think, feel and do is *directly* related to outer conditions. As a result, extraverts adapt easily to external situations, although as a result they are also rather suggestible and changeable. They generally come across as outgoing, venturesome, confident, approachable and sociable people who readily form new interests and attachments. In their enthusiasm for the outside world, however, extraverts usually ignore subjective experiences. For this reason they are often cheerfully unaware of inner, psychological processes.

Attitudinal relationships

Although each individual will tend, consciously, to be either introverted or extraverted, every person is believed to have the potential to express both attitudes. Generally speaking, the dominant (conscious) attitude will be compensated by its inferior (unconscious) opposite.

To the extent that the opposite attitude type remains unconscious it will, in moments of intoxication, difficulty or distress, spontaneously express itself in inferior, maladjusted, compulsive or infantile ways. Thus the drunken, disturbed or neurotic extravert may become sullen, withdrawn and egocentric, whereas the introvert in these circumstances may be childishly sociable, giddy and overexcitable. Alternatively, these negative characteristics may be projected onto people of the opposite attitude type. In this way the extravert may accuse introverts of being sullen and egocentric, while the introvert may see extraverts as childish and silly. Such projections, it may be said, provide the foundations of many family, marital and other interpersonal conflicts.

PSYCHOLOGICAL TYPES

Putting together the two attitude and eight function types produces a final model in which there are sixteen possible outcomes. These sixteen psychological types are shown in Table 5.

Table 5 The sixteen Jungian psychological types

'Pure' types	

Extraverted Sensation	Introverted Sensation
Extraverted Intuition	Introverted Intuition
Extraverted Thinking	Introverted Thinking
Extraverted Feeling	Introverted Feeling

'Mixed' types	

Extraverted Sensory Thinking	Introverted Sensory Thinking
Extraverted Sensory Feeling	Introverted Sensory Feeling
Extraverted Intuitive Thinking	Introverted Intuitive Thinking
Extraverted Intuitive Feeling	Introverted Intuitive Feeling

Jung himself discusses in detail only the eight 'pure' types (i.e., the combinations of attitude and *single* function). An understanding of the 'mixed' types (where *two* functions are operating simultaneously) is believed to be derivable from a knowledge of the two component types. For example, the extraverted sensory thinking type is basically a mixture of the extraverted sensation and extraverted thinking types.

The extraverted sensation type

Extraverted sensation strives for intensity of experience derived from concrete objects and physical activities. Consciousness is therefore directed outward to those objects and activities that may be expected to arouse the strongest sensations.

The extraverted sensation type is a realist who seeks to experience as many concrete sensations as possible – preferably, but not necessarily, ones that are pleasurable. These experiences are seen as ends in themselves and are rarely utilized for any other purpose. If normal, such persons are sensualists or aesthetes who are attracted by the physical characteristics of objects and people. They dress, eat and entertain well, and can be very good company. Not at all reflective nor introspective, they have no ideals except sensory enjoyment. They generally mistrust inner psychological processes and prefer to account for such things in terms of external events (e.g., they may blame their moods on the weather). If extreme, they are often crudely sensual and may exploit situations or others in order to increase their own personal pleasure. When neurotic, repressed intuition may be projected onto other people, so that they may become irrationally suspicious or jealous. Alternatively, they may develop a range of compulsive superstitions.

The introverted sensation type

Introverted sensation is subjectively filtered. Perception is not based directly on the object, but is merely suggested by it. Instead, layers of subjective impressions are superimposed upon the image so that it becomes impossible to determine what will be perceived from a knowledge only of the object. Perception thus depends crucially upon internal psychological processes that will differ from one person to the next. At its most positive, introverted sensation is found in the creative artist. At its most extreme, it produces psychotic hallucinations and a total alienation from reality.

The introverted sensation type reacts subjectively to events in a way that is unrelated to objective criteria. Often this is seen as an inappropriate and uncalled-for overreaction. Because objects generally fail to penetrate directly the veil of subjective impressions, this type may seem neutral or indifferent to objective reality. Alternatively, the person may perceive the world as illusory or amusing. In extreme (psychotic) cases, this may result in an inability to distinguish illusion from reality. The subjective world of archaic images may then come to dominate consciousness completely, so that the person lives in a private, mythological realm of fantasy. Repressed intuition may also be expressed in vaguely imagined threats or an apprehension of sinister possibilities.

The extraverted intuition type

Extraverted intuition attempts to envisage all the possibilities that are inherent in an objective situation. Ordinary events are seen as providing a cipher or set of clues from which underlying processes and hidden potentialities can be determined. Yet once these possibilities are apprehended, objects and events lose their meaning and import. There is therefore a constant need for new situations and experiences to provide a fresh stimulus for the intuitive process.

The extraverted intuition type is an excellent diagnostician and exploiter of situations. Such people see exciting possibilities in every new venture and are excellent at perceiving latent abilities in other people. They get carried away with the enthusiasm of their vision and often inspire others with their courage and conviction. As such, they do well in occupations where these qualities are at a premium – for example in initiating new projects, in business, politics or the stock market. They are, however, easily bored and stifled by unchanging conditions. As a result they often waste their life and talents jumping from one activity to another in the search for fresh possibilities, failing to stick at any one project long enough to bring it to fruition. Furthermore, in their commitment to their own vision, they often show little regard for the needs, views or convictions of others. When neurotic, repressed sensation may cause this type to become compulsively tied to people, objects or activities that stir in them primitive sensations such as pleasure, pain or fear. The consequence of this can be phobias, hypochondriacal beliefs and a range of other compulsions.

The introverted intuition type

Introverted intuition is directed inward to the contents of the unconscious. It attempts to fathom internal events by relating them to universal psychological processes or to other archetypal images. Consequently it generally has a mythical, symbolic or prophetic quality.

According to Jung, the introverted intuition type can be either an artist, seer or crank. Such a person has a visionary ideal that reveals strange, mysterious things. These are enigmatic, 'unearthly' people who stand aloof from ordinary society. They have little interest in explaining or rationalizing their personal vision, but are content merely to proclaim it. Partly as a result of this, they are often misunderstood. Although the vision of the artist among this type generally remains on the purely perceptual level, mystical dreamers or cranks may become caught up in theirs. The person's life then becomes symbolic, taking on the nature of a Great Work, mission or spiritual-moral quest. If neurotic, repressed sensation may express itself in primitive, instinctual ways and, like their extraverted counterparts, introverted intuitives often suffer from hypochondria and compulsions.

The extraverted thinking type

Extraverted thinking is driven by the objective evidence of the senses or by objective (collective) ideas that derive from tradition or learning. Its purpose is to abstract conceptual relationships from objective experience, linking ideas together in a rational, logical fashion. Furthermore, any conclusions that are drawn are always directed outward to some objective product or practical outcome. Thinking is never carried out for its own sake, merely as some private, subjective enterprise.

The extraverted thinking type bases all actions on the intellectual analysis of objective data. Such people live by a general intellectual formula or universal moral code, founded upon abstract notions of truth or justice. They also expect other people to recognize and obey this formula. This type represses the feeling function (e.g., sentimental attachments, friendships, religious devotion) and may also neglect personal interests such as their own health or financial well-being. If extreme or neurotic, they may become petty, bigoted, tyrannical or hostile towards those who would threaten their formula. Alternatively, repressed tendencies may burst out in various kinds of personal 'immorality' (e.g., self-seeking, sexual misdemeanours, fraud or deception).

The introverted thinking type

Introverted thinking is contemplative, involving an inner play of ideas. It is thinking for its own sake and is always directed inward to subjective ideas and personal convictions rather than outward to practical outcomes. The main concern of such thinking is to elaborate as fully as possible all the ramifications and implications of a seminal idea. As a consequence, introverted thinking can be complex, turgid and overly scrupulous. To the extent that it withdraws from objective reality, it may also become totally abstract, symbolic or mystical.

The introverted thinking type tends to be impractical and indifferent to objective concerns. These persons usually avoid notice and may seem cold, arrogant and taciturn. Alternatively, the repressed feeling function may express itself in displays of childish naivety. Generally people of this type appear caught up in their own ideas which they aim to think through as fully and deeply as possible. If extreme or neurotic they can become rigid, withdrawn, surly or brusque. They may also confuse their subjectively apprehended truth with their own personality so that any criticism of their ideas is seen as a personal attack. This may lead to bitterness or to vicious counterattacks against their critics.

The extraverted feeling type

Extraverted feeling is based upon accepted or traditional social values and opinions. It involves a conforming, adjusting response to objective circumstances that strives for harmonious relations with the world. Because it depends so much on external stimuli rather than upon true subjective preferences, such feeling can sometimes seem cold, 'unfeeling', artificial or put on for effect.

The extraverted feeling type follows fashion and seeks to harmonize personal feelings with general social values. Thinking is always subordinate to feeling and is ignored or repressed if intellectual conclusions fail to confirm the convictions of the heart. When this type is extreme or neurotic, feeling may become gushing or extravagant and dependent upon momentary enthusiasms that may quickly turn about with changing circumstances. Such a person may therefore seem hysterical, fickle, moody or even to be suffering from multiple personality. Repressed thinking may also erupt in infantile, negative, obsessive ways. This can lead to the attribution of dreaded characteristics to the very objects or people that are most loved and valued.

The introverted feeling type

Introverted feeling strives for an inner intensity that is unrelated to any external object. It devalues objective reality and is rarely displayed openly.

When it does appear on the surface it generally seems negative or indifferent. The focus of such feeling is upon inner processes and latent, primordial images. At its extreme, it may develop into mystical ecstasy.

The introverted feeling type is brooding and inaccessible, although may also hide behind a childish mask. Such a person aims to be inconspicuous, makes little attempt to impress and generally fails to respond to the feelings of others. The outer, surface appearance is often neutral, cold and dismissive. Inwardly, however, feelings are deep, passionately intense, and may accompany secret religious or poetic tendencies. The effect of all this on other people can be stifling and oppressive. When extreme or neurotic, this type may become domineering and vain. Negative repressed thinking may also be projected so that these persons may imagine they can know what others are thinking. This may develop into paranoia and into secret scheming rivalries.

ASSESSING TYPES

In order to determine psychological types from a Watchword matrix it is necessary simply to consider the kinds of words written at each key location. In practice this will be found much easier, clearer and generally more reliable than attempts to assess directly the psychological processes underlying the formation of specific connections. To begin, you should consider the *function* of consciousness (i.e., sensation, intuition, thinking or feeling) implied by each of the eleven *key* words. When this has been decided, you may examine the psychological *attitude* that seems to dominate the matrix (i.e., introversion or extraversion). The following general principles will be found helpful when distinguishing functions and attitudes.

General principles

Sensation is suggested when key words refer to concrete objects (e.g., 'car', 'book', 'shoe') or to purely physical or sensory experiences (e.g., 'hunger', 'hot', 'black'). There should be no strong evidence of an emotional or sentimental attraction (repulsion) towards these objects or experiences. Also there should be no clear indication of psychological metaphor or symbolism. Even though a major assumption of the Watchword technique is that seemingly banal, concrete words can represent or symbolize deeper psychological processes, such a possibility should not be immediately apparent to the casual observer.

Intuition is often the most difficult of the four functions to identify in the Watchword matrix. It is implicated when words reveal a recognition or interpretation of basic processes and inherent possibilities. It thus involves a deeper appreciation of reality than does sensation. Generally it points to underlying social or psychological phenomena, profound human experiences or fundamental drives and motives. There is also invariably some indication that the individual is personally and creatively involved with these processes and possibilities to a degree that goes beyond a purely conceptual understanding or straightforward sentimental reaction. Examples of intuitive words are 'creation', 'sacrifice', 'fulfilment', 'growth', 'decision', 'faith' and 'ambition.'

Thinking is suggested by words at key locations which are analytical, abstract and conceptual (e.g., 'reading', 'majority', 'foreign', 'similar', 'structure', 'collection'). Such words are generally emotionally neutral or, if emotional, seem to imply a conceptual understanding of the affective dimension rather than an actual feeling response (e.g., 'punishment' rather than 'hurt', 'altruism' rather than 'help', 'attachment' rather than 'boy-friend'). Also there should be no clear indication that concepts have been derived from a deeper probing of reality that attempts to identify funda-mental underlying processes or possibilities (cf. intuition).

Feeling is indicated when key words reflect a personal emotional reaction or sentimental response to the object, person or concept mentioned (e.g., 'mother', 'upset', 'sex', 'dirt', 'happy', 'pet'). The words always clearly imply a sense of liking or dislike (pleasantness or unpleasant-ness) which should dominate any other considerations.

Introversion is suggested when key words refer to private, intimate, uncommunicated experience, or to the inner, psychological dimension (e.g., 'studying', 'despair', 'silence', 'hidden', 'sleep', 'thoughts'). There is little reference to, or sense of connection with, the outside world of physical and social events. Instead the words generally imply an attitude of self-absorption and insularity.

Extraversion is indicated when the words point outward to (or suggest communication with) the physical or social environments (e.g., 'party', 'holiday', 'town', 'colleague', 'outburst', 'telephone'). Even though the matrix may mention thoughts, feelings or psychological processes, these are always clearly related to external events, physical objects or shared beliefs.

Mixed and ambivalent types

It is unusual for a Watchword matrix to reflect only one of the four func-tions. More commonly a matrix will suggest two (possibly three) functions, although usually one of these will dominate. Such mixed types are indicated when the matrix contains some key words that suggest one function together with other key words that suggest a different function. Alternatively, individual key words sometimes suggest two functions (e.g., 'flat' and 'warm' imply both sensation and feeling).

Interestingly, the Watchword technique gives considerable support for Jung's belief in the two pairs of opposite functions. It is therefore rare to find combinations of thinking and feeling, or of sensation and intuition. Instead most combinations can be readily identified with the mixed types implied in Jung's theory (i.e., sensory thinking, intuitive thinking, sensory feeling and intuitive feeling).

The distinction between introversion and extraversion is often less clear-cut. Thus many matrices indicate a fairly ambivalent (ambivert) attitude, containing elements of both introversion and extraversion. In spite of this it will usually be possible to identify one attitude as the more dominant, enabling the final psychological type to be determined.

LEARNING TO TYPE WATCHWORD MATRICES

The best way to learn to type a Watchword matrix is by examining examples. To begin with, it is useful to simplify matters by considering only the eight basic single-attitude and single-function types. Once you are familiar with the characteristics of these 'pure' types it becomes a much easier task to assess the more problematical ambivert and mixed-function matrices. For this reason the following sections present example matrices for each of the eight basic Jungian types. These should be studied carefully until the rationale for these classifications becomes clear. It should be noted that all matrices are genuine examples; they have not been artificially constructed as teaching aids. This means that even though the dominant attitude and function are fairly clear in all cases, several matrices show traces of the other attitude or of other functions. This reflects the point made earlier that truly 'pure', unmixed types are quite rare.

The extraverted sensation type

Extraverted sensation is normally indicated by a set of key words that refer to everyday concrete objects, sensory experiences or physical activities. There is no obvious sense of symbolism in the words used; neither is there any indication that their meanings are coloured or influenced by personal, subjective factors. Instead there is usually an apparent banality in the matrix that argues against the attempt to read into it any kind of psychological significance. At times the matrix clearly suggests a nature that is simple, uncomplicated and orientated towards sensory enjoyment. Occasionally, however, there may be references to unpleasant sensations (rather than feelings) such as boredom, drunkenness, sickness, stenches, noise or burning.

Matrices 1–4 are typical examples of extraverted sensation. Matrix 1 is a good illustration of Watchword at its apparently most banal and insignificant. Matrices 2 and 3 reveal the pleasure-seeking aspect of extraverted sensation (although both also recognize unpleasant sensations). Finally, Matrix 4 indicates an orientation towards intense sensation for its own sake, unrelated to pleasure.

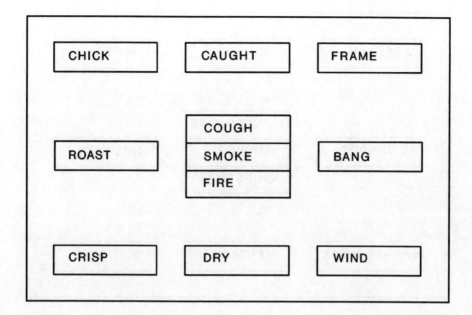

Matrix 1

Matrix 2

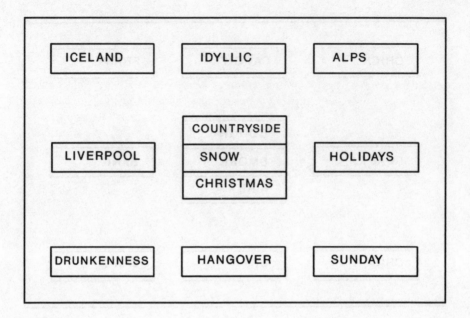

Matrix 3

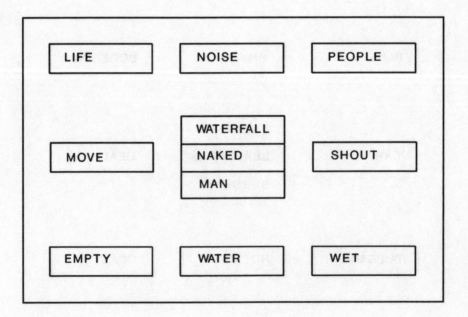

Matrix 4

The introverted sensation type

It can be quite difficult to distinguish introverted from extraverted sensation in the Watchword matrix, since both typically refer to concrete objects or sensory experiences. In general terms, however, introverted sensation always appears more intimate, personal or private than extraverted sensation. The words chosen are also often more imaginative and idiosyncratic than those of the extraverted sensation type. The impression given is that objects mentioned have quite strong subjective associations, while experiences are generally those that are best appreciated alone. There may also be a dreamlike, fantastic or illusory quality to the matrix.

Matrices 5–8 are typical examples of introverted sensation. Matrix 5 shows something of the intimacy often associated with this type, while Matrix 6 is more imaginative and seemingly more archaic. Matrix 7, on the other hand, focuses directly upon the individual's private sensory experience. Finally, Matrix 8 hints at the potentially illusory, fantastic, alienated and purely subjective nature of introverted sensation.

The extraverted intuition type

Extraverted intuition is indicated when key words refer to possibilities that are inherent in outer (generally social) experience, to underlying social processes or to fundamental outward-looking drives and motivations. This

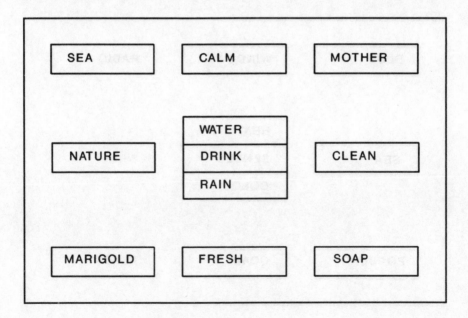

Matrix 5

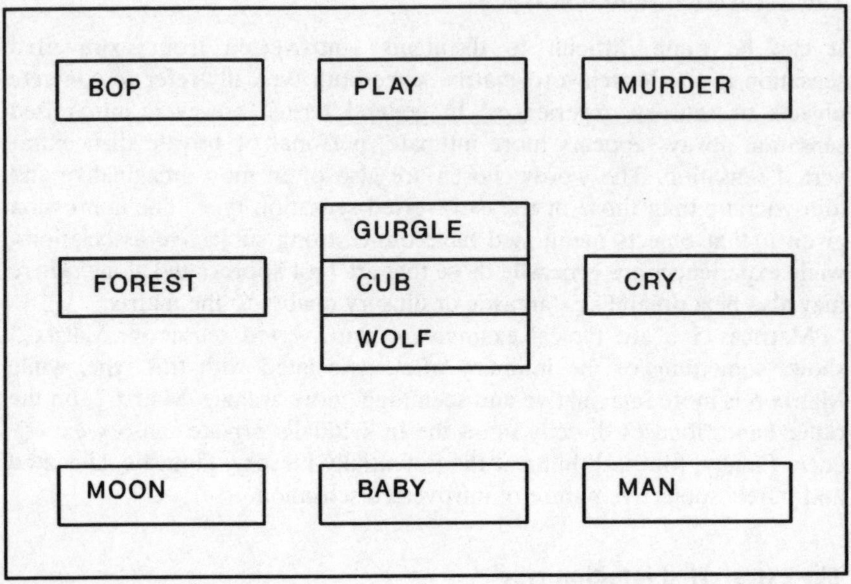

BOP	PLAY	MURDER
FOREST	GURGLE CUB WOLF	CRY
MOON	BABY	MAN

Matrix 6

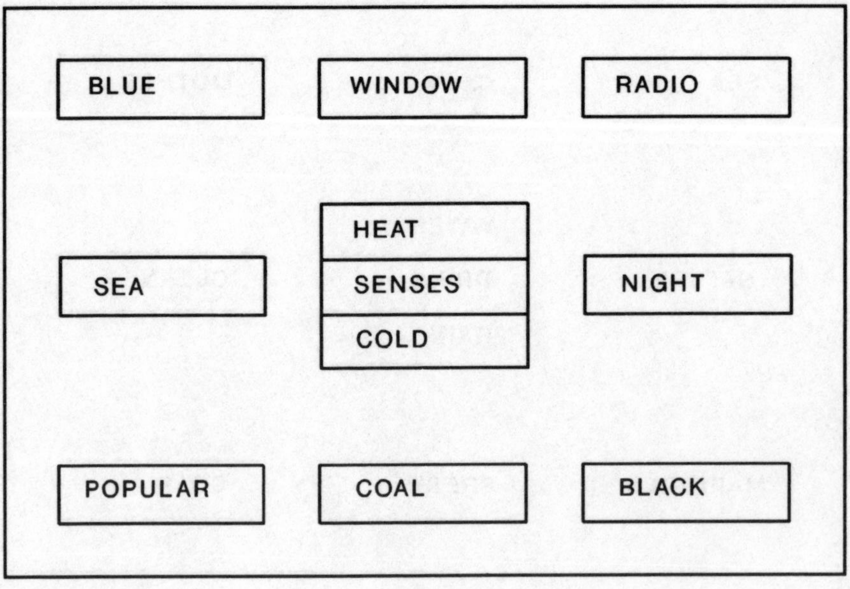

BLUE	WINDOW	RADIO
SEA	HEAT SENSES COLD	NIGHT
POPULAR	COAL	BLACK

Matrix 7

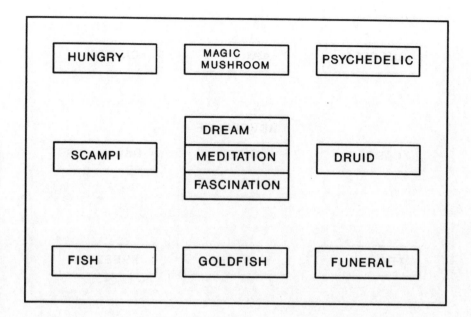

Matrix 8

involves much more than a purely conceptual analysis of the world. Instead there should be a clear sense that the person is interpreting outer reality in terms of his or her own basic purposes, i.e., is 'reading in' meanings that another person might not recognize. For this reason the key words always seem personally significant, reflecting a strong degree of individual commitment and involvement. They are never simply abstract and neutral.

Extraverted intuition is commonly orientated towards personal advancement or the achievement of success and happiness in the world. This is often linked to the individual's career, to a sense of vocation or to the development of family and friendships. Other typical expressions of extraverted intuition involve the recognition of challenge or the need for personal change, decision or action.

Matrices 9–12 are typical examples of extraverted intuition. Matrix 9 is a good illustration of the career-orientated type. Matrix 10 focuses upon the need to develop relationships and the public personality. Matrix 11 recognizes present conflicts and emphasizes the need for decision and change. Matrix 12 is more complex, but again points to the importance of change in response to the personal challenge presented by current confusion and difficulties.

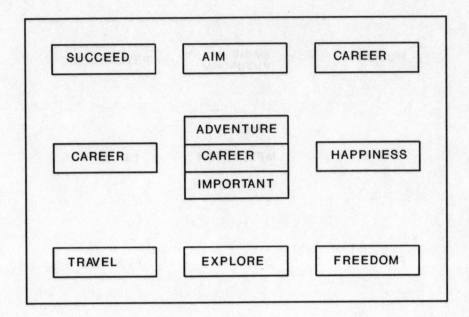

Matrix 9

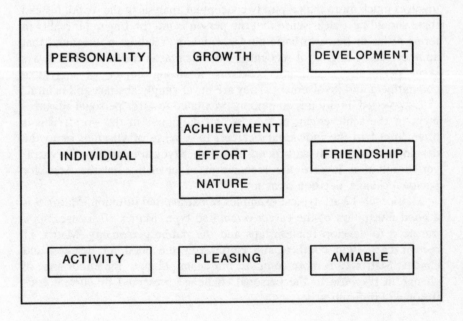

Matrix 10

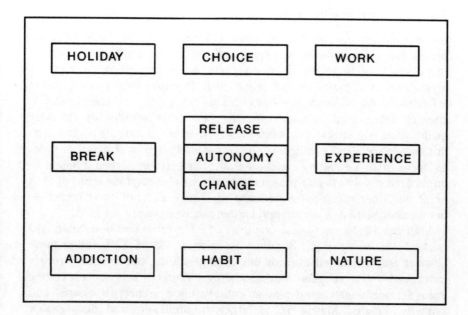

Matrix 11

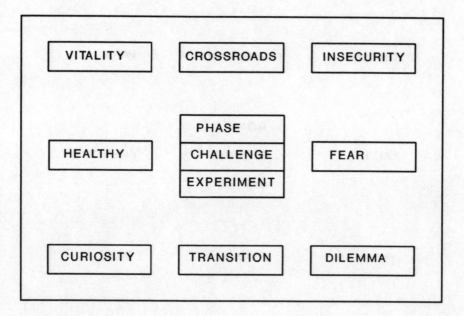

Matrix 12

The introverted intuition type

Introverted intuition, in its pure form, is rarely found in the Watchword matrix. It is indicated when key words refer to fundamental inner processes of personal development. Typically these are expressed in the form of mysterious, archetypal images (e.g., God, Buddha, Hero) or by direct reference to the universal absolutes of inner being (e.g., existence, mind or energy). Introverted intuition often has an 'other worldly' or visionary quality that is unmistakable when observed in the matrix. It is, however, not always specifically 'religious' in the generally accepted sense; at times its focus may be purely psychological. Furthermore, when religion is implied, this is always interpreted mystically – for example in terms of faith or of the inner numinous experience of God – and not by reference to outer manifestations such as church attendance or charity work.

Matrices 13–16 are typical examples of introverted intuition. Matrix 13 is clearly based upon the Buddhist experience. Matrix 14 is rather more abstract and orientated towards universal absolutes, but is again strongly influenced by a religious understanding. Matrix 15 is an interesting example, seemingly based almost entirely upon archetypal images and symbols. Finally, Matrix 16 is largely nonreligious and nonsymbolic but focuses instead directly upon the inner processes of psychological development.

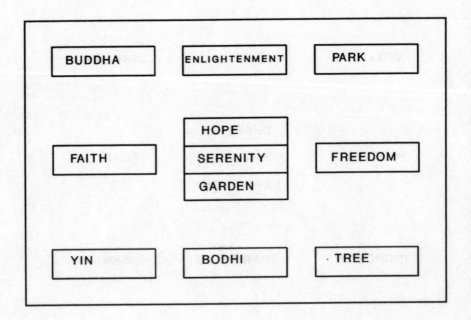

Matrix 13

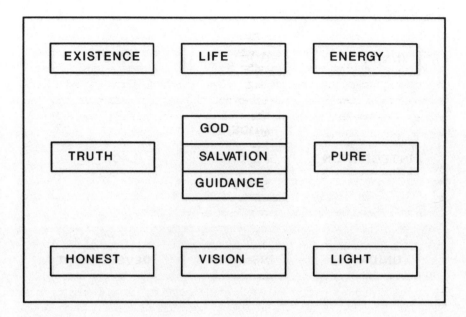

Matrix 14

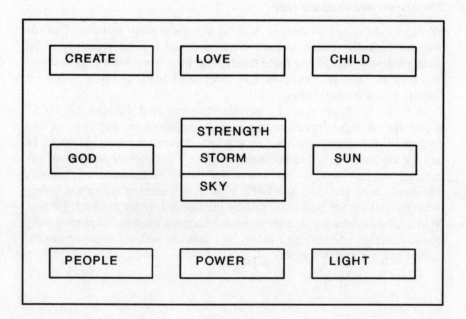

Matrix 15

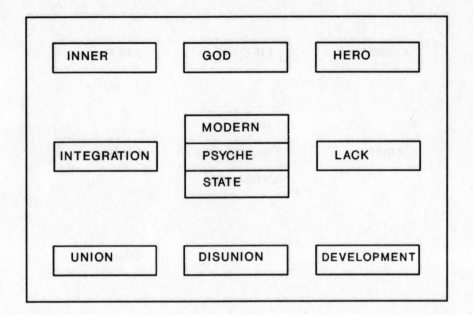

Matrix 16

The extraverted thinking type

Matrices exhibiting extraverted thinking usually contain a series of words that are logically related to each other and which seem primarily to be concerned with identifying basic conceptual principles. Furthermore these concepts are always rooted in and orientated towards outer events or collective (traditional) beliefs.

Matrices 17–20 are typical examples of extraverted thinking. Matrix 17 is perhaps the most representative case, being almost totally abstract and conceptual yet at the same time clearly linked to outer events. Matrices 18 and 19 are more concrete but again suggest a conceptual analysis of the external environment. It may be noted that the mention of 'babies', 'children', 'relations', etc., in Matrix 19 does not seem to indicate a *feeling* response but rather implies a purely intellectual understanding. Finally, Matrix 20 is interesting because it provides a good example of ideologically bound extraverted thinking (not to be confused with an intuitive understanding of societal processes).

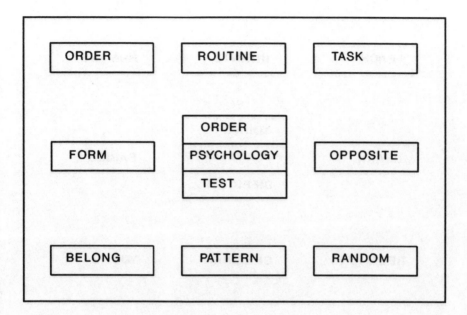

```
┌──────────────────────────────────────────────────────┐
│                                                        │
│   ┌──────────┐      ┌──────────┐      ┌──────────┐     │
│   │  ORDER   │      │ ROUTINE  │      │   TASK   │     │
│   └──────────┘      └──────────┘      └──────────┘     │
│                     ┌──────────┐                       │
│                     │  ORDER   │                       │
│   ┌──────────┐      ├──────────┤      ┌──────────┐     │
│   │   FORM   │      │PSYCHOLOGY│      │ OPPOSITE │     │
│   └──────────┘      ├──────────┤      └──────────┘     │
│                     │   TEST   │                       │
│                     └──────────┘                       │
│   ┌──────────┐      ┌──────────┐      ┌──────────┐     │
│   │  BELONG  │      │ PATTERN  │      │  RANDOM  │     │
│   └──────────┘      └──────────┘      └──────────┘     │
│                                                        │
└──────────────────────────────────────────────────────┘
```

Matrix 17

```
┌──────────────────────────────────────────────────────┐
│                                                        │
│   ┌──────────┐      ┌──────────┐      ┌──────────┐     │
│   │ MESSAGE  │      │ SOCIALIZE│      │  RULER   │     │
│   └──────────┘      └──────────┘      └──────────┘     │
│                     ┌──────────┐                       │
│                     │  MEDIA   │                       │
│   ┌──────────┐      ├──────────┤      ┌──────────┐     │
│   │TELEPHONE │      │COMMUNICATE│     │ COUNTRY  │     │
│   └──────────┘      ├──────────┤      └──────────┘     │
│                     │INTERNATIONAL│                    │
│                     └──────────┘                       │
│   ┌──────────┐      ┌──────────┐      ┌──────────┐     │
│   │COMMUNICATE│     │  PEOPLE  │      │   KING   │     │
│   └──────────┘      └──────────┘      └──────────┘     │
│                                                        │
└──────────────────────────────────────────────────────┘
```

Matrix 18

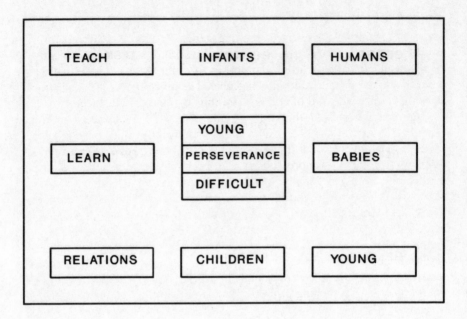

Matrix 19

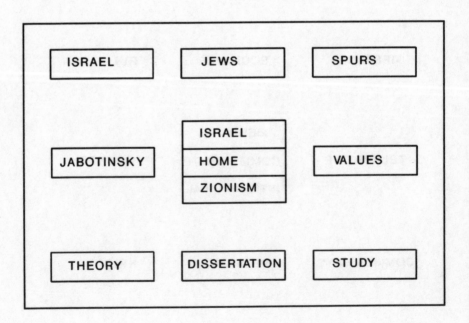

Matrix 20

The introverted thinking type

Matrices exhibiting introverted thinking generally give the impression of abstract thinking that is carried out for its own sake, as a purely subjective exercise, and that bears little relationship to outer events. These matrices typically appear obscure and impenetrable. They may indeed be so abstract as to seem totally devoid of content and thus without significance.

Unmixed introverted thinking is quite rare in a Watchword matrix. However, Matrices 21–24 give a fairly good indication of this type. Matrices 21 and 22 show the abstract, content-free nature of introverted thinking. Matrix 23 is more substantial, revealing a strong sense of inner intellectual confusion. Finally, Matrix 24 is a fascinating example (as also is Matrix 22) of how introverted thinking can become totally cramped in its obsessive concern with elaborating a particular subjective idea. It should be noted that Matrix 24 does not implicate the *feeling* function even though its major reference is to the affective dimension. This is because the primary emphasis in the matrix seems to be with the identification of conceptual interrelationships between emotional concepts. The person thus appears to be thinking about feeling rather than demonstrating an actual feeling response.

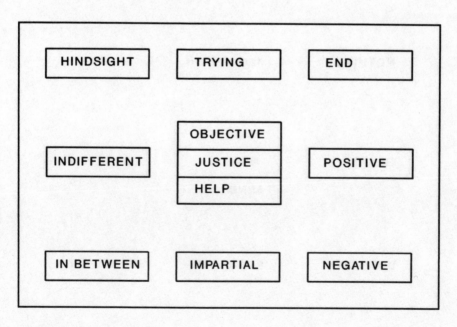

Matrix 21

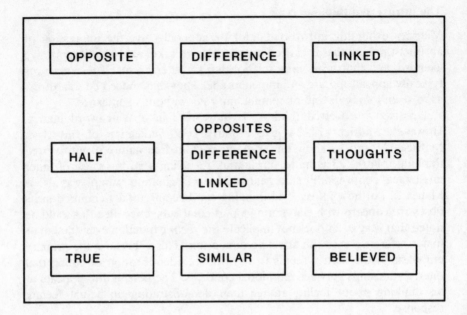

Matrix 22

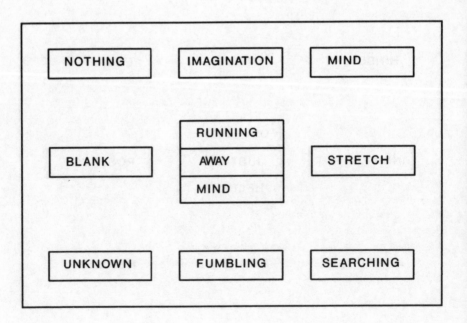

Matrix 23

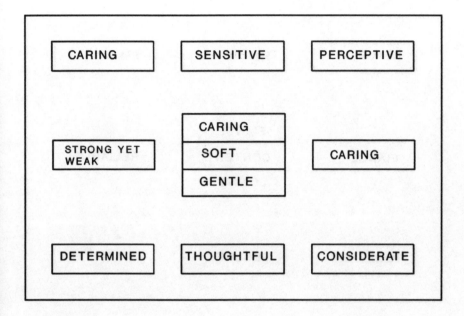

Matrix 24

The extraverted feeling type

Extraverted feeling is indicated when key words suggest an emotional or sentimental reaction that can be related directly to outer circumstances or accepted values. The basic response is therefore one in which feelings are adjusted to fit the situation. Commonly found, extraverted feeling may be exhibited in several different forms. Partly these depend upon the basic emotional tone of the matrix. Thus some matrices indicate a happy, contented, well-adjusted nature, whereas others seem to be dominated by powerful or disturbed emotions such as anger, anxiety or depression. In all cases, however, these feelings can clearly be seen as reactions to external events rather than as reflecting purely subjective tendencies.

Matrices 25–28 are typical examples of extraverted feeling. Matrix 25 shows the happy, well-adjusted type. Matrix 26 reveals a somewhat depressed response to the problems of relationships, while Matrix 27 suggests anxiety related to family life, sex and health. Finally, Matrix 28 indicates a degree of anger or cynicism connected with the troubles in Northern Ireland.

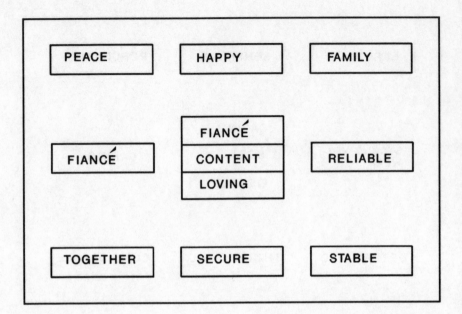

Matrix 25

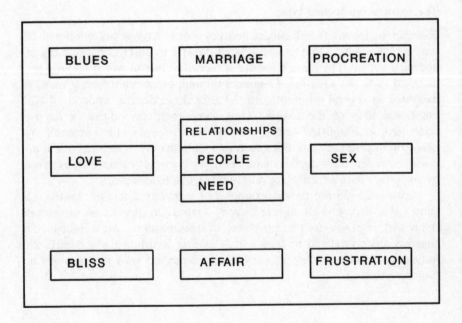

Matrix 26

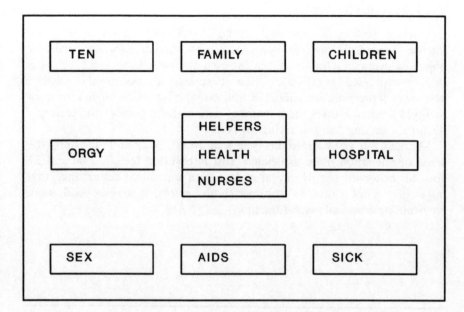

Matrix 27

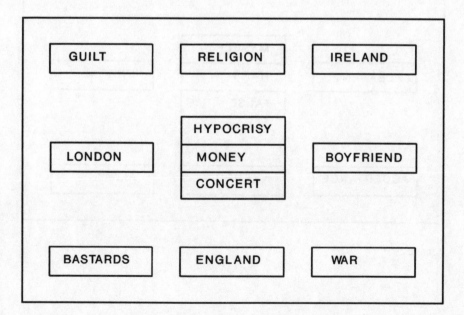

Matrix 28

The introverted feeling type

Introverted feeling is expressed in the Watchword matrix in terms of intense, apparently raw emotion that seems unrelated to any particular object or event. As Jung noted in his own analysis of this type, feeling is usually expressed negatively. Often it appears as nonspecific anxiety, brooding depression, emotional confusion or a sense of alienation from reality. In extreme cases these matrices may reveal a person who is deeply disturbed, sinking fast and crying for help.

Matrices 29–32 illustrate this type well. Matrices 29 and 30 exhibit the sense of alienation often associated with introverted feeling. Matrices 31 and 32, however, clearly reveal a degree of emotional disturbance that might give some cause for concern (both people, it may be said, were receiving professional help at the time).

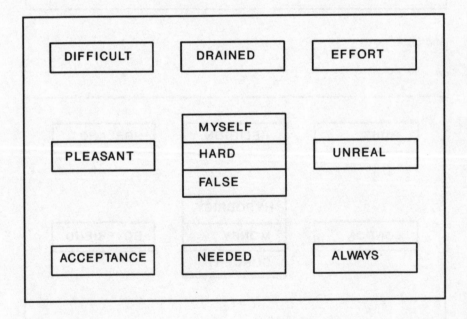

Matrix 29

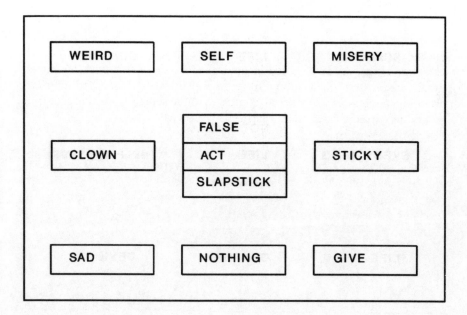

Matrix 30

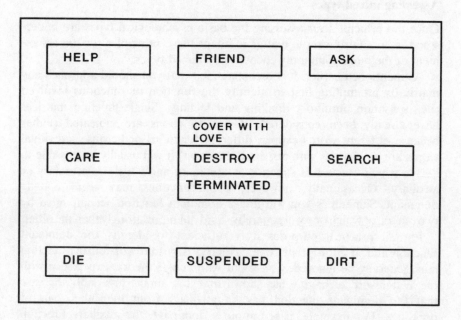

Matrix 31

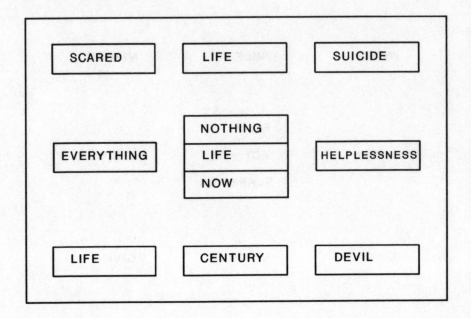

Matrix 32

Assessing mixed types

Once the principles for assessing the basic psychological types are understood, it is a fairly simple matter to adapt these principles for the assessment of the more commonly encountered mixed types.

As mentioned earlier, it is recommended that you should approach any matrix by attempting first to identify the function or functions involved (i.e., sensation, intuition, thinking and feeling). Single-function matrices have already been considered. If two functions are indicated (either because different words express different functions or because individual words are ambiguous with respect to function) it will usually be possible to decide which function is superior or dominant and which is secondary or auxiliary. Occasionally, however, both functions may seem equally dominant. Sometimes you will find a dominant function accompanied by two others, of which one will generally stand out more strongly than the other.

For all practical purposes it is sufficient to identify the dominant function and, if appropriate, one auxiliary. Any third (or fourth) function may generally be ignored. Consistent with Jung's theory, experience with the Watchword technique has shown that it is almost invariably the case that the dominant function has an auxiliary from the other pair of opposites. For example, if sensation is dominant, the auxiliary function may be thinking or feeling but never intuition. Similarly, feeling may be accompanied by sensation or intuition but not by thinking.

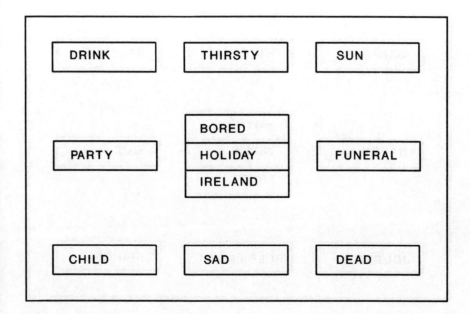

Matrix 33

It is useful to describe function types using a standard notational system. Following the lead of the Myers-Briggs Type Indicator (Myers and McCaulley, 1985), each function is represented by an initial, i.e., S (sensation), N (intuition), T (thinking) and F (feeling). To describe mixed matrices, the dominant function is written first, followed in brackets by the auxiliary function. Thus S(F) indicates the sensory feeling type with sensation dominant, whereas F(S) denotes the same type but with feeling as the dominant function. When the two functions seem equally dominant, the two letters follow each other without brackets. Thus ST indicates a balanced sensory thinking type, and NF a balanced intuitive feeling type.

Having determined the function type, the matrix may be examined in terms of attitude (introversion or extraversion). Even though many matrices show both attitudes in some measure, it is usually possible to decide which attitude is dominant. Occasionally, however, a matrix may appear to exhibit both attitudes almost equally. In such cases the matrix may usefully be described as *ambivert*.

In order to denote the attitude types, the letters I (introversion), E (extraversion) and A (ambiversion) are used. These may then be combined with the function notation to provide a full description of psychological type. Thus IS(T) indicates the introverted sensory thinking type (sensation dominant), EN(F) denotes the extraverted intuitive feeling type (intuition dominant) and AF describes the ambivert feeling type.

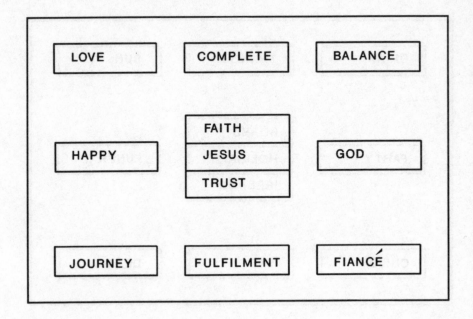

Matrix 34

To illustrate the typing of mixed matrices, a few examples should suffice (Matrices 33–38).

Matrix 33 is dominated by sensation or sensory feeling ('drink', 'thirsty', 'sun', 'party', 'bored', 'holiday', 'Ireland', 'child') with a minority of words that are more specifically feeling ('funeral', 'sad', 'dead'). In general, the sensation function appears to be stronger than feeling. Since the attitude indicated in the matrix is clearly extraverted, the psychological type may be described as extraverted sensory feeling. An appropriate notation for this matrix would be ES(F).

Matrix 34 exhibits a strongly intuitive or intuitive feeling function ('love', 'complete', 'balance', 'faith', 'Jesus', 'God', 'trust', 'journey', 'fulfilment'). In addition, there are two words that are more directly feeling ('happy', 'fiancé'). The overall impression is that intuition is more salient than feeling. The attitude involved in this matrix is generally introverted and therefore the psychological type may be described as introverted intuitive feeling. An appropriate notation would be IN(F).

Matrix 35 reveals a combination of sensation ('hop', 'play', 'fun', 'stamp'), sensory thinking ('scenes', 'articles', 'report', 'applause') and thinking ('approval', 'safety', 'subsets'). The relative strengths of sensation and thinking appear fairly evenly balanced, with possibly a slight leaning towards thinking. The extraverted attitude is dominant and therefore the matrix indicates the extraverted sensory thinking type. Depending upon the

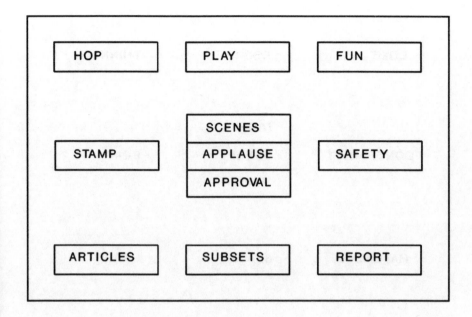

Matrix 35

relative balance that is attributed to sensation and thinking, the matrix could be meaningfully denoted as either ET(S) or EST.

Matrix 36 includes five sensation or sensory feeling words ('room', 'night', 'sleep', 'black', 'crash'), four feeling words ('comfort', 'happy', 'fear', 'hate mail') and two thinking words ('think', 'contradict'). Since thinking is clearly a minor function, it may be ignored for the purposes of psychological typing. The two remaining functions (sensation and feeling) seem almost equally dominant, although perhaps feeling is slightly stronger. The attitude in this matrix is introverted and the psychological type may therefore be described as introverted sensory feeling. An appropriate notation would be ISF or IF(S).

Matrix 37 shows a predominance of sensation words ('pub', 'money', 'bank', 'psychedelic', 'drug', 'machine', 'sleep', 'dream', 'night') with two apparently thinking words ('closed', 'open'). More interesting, however, is the clearly ambivalent psychological attitude that is exhibited in the matrix. Thus there seems to be an almost equal split between introversion ('closed', 'sleep', 'dream', 'night') and extraversion ('pub', 'money', 'bank', 'machine', 'open'). The words 'psychedelic' and 'drug' could reflect either introversion or extraversion. An ambivert sensation or sensory thinking type is therefore indicated. Notation for this matrix could be either AS or AS(T).

Matrix 38 indicates a strong feeling function ('mood', 'lonesome', 'unhappy', 'ill', 'impotent', 'frigid') with other words suggesting intuition or

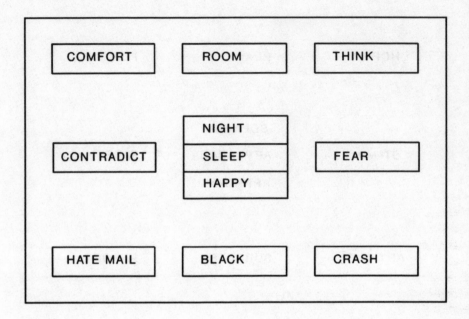

Matrix 36

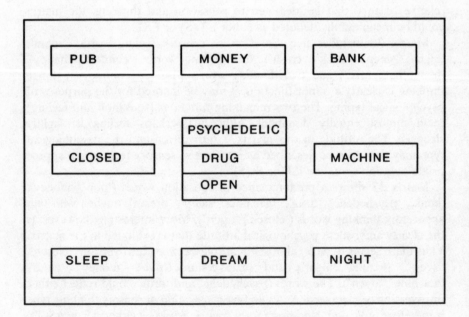

Matrix 37

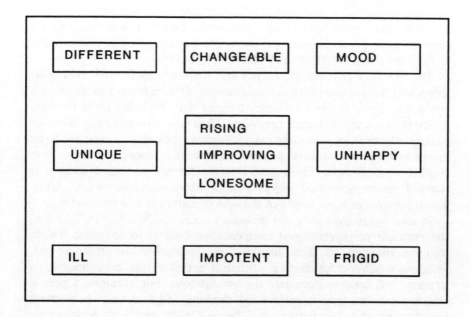

Matrix 38

intuitive thinking ('changeable', 'rising', 'improving', 'unique'). Finally, there is one more specifically thinking word ('different'). In terms of relative strengths, feeling seems to be the dominant function, with intuition second. Thinking is the third function and may therefore be ignored. The attitude reflected in the matrix is essentially introverted, indicating the introverted intuitive feeling type. An appropriate notation for the matrix would be IF(N).

PERSONAL SIGNIFICANCE OF PSYCHOLOGICAL TYPE

Awareness of one's psychological type is important for several reasons. Most significantly it helps us to understand and differentiate our own conscious tendencies. According to Jung one of the major tasks of the first half of life is to learn to express effectively our dominant function and attitude. Many people, however, are quite uncertain about their psychological type. This lack of awareness may cause problems of adjustment, particularly in terms of career aspirations or relationships with others. The Watchword technique may be especially useful for such people.

With respect to career, there is no doubt that certain types are theoretically suited or unsuited to particular occupations. For example, an extraverted intuitive type might be expected to do well in business, management or politics but poorly, say, as a tea-taster or impressionist painter. Similarly, an introverted thinking type might make an excellent mathematician or library assistant but would probably find difficulty functioning as a nurse or social worker. In considering how alternative career choices relate to the person's basic psychological type, more effective decisions may be possible in this area (see also, Myers and McCaulley, 1985).

The theory of psychological types also helps to explain how incompatibility and friction can occur between people. One important cause of such problems can be the lack of understanding that inevitably exists to some extent between psychological opposites. Thus introverts can have difficulty in their relationships with extraverts, sensation types may be expected to be misunderstood by intuitive persons and feeling types may come into conflict with thinkers. These problems are further magnified when it is realized that persons may project their negative, undifferentiated, unconscious proclivities onto people of the opposite attitude and function type.

In addition to indicating our dominant conscious function and attitude, the principle of psychological compensation enables us to obtain insight into the direction of these unconscious tendencies. According to this principle whichever function or attitude is uppermost in consciousness, its opposite will tend to dominate the unconscious. For example, a person whose conscious type is extraverted thinking will find that unconscious impulses express introversion and feeling, although in a primitive or infantile manner (see the descriptions of the basic psychological types presented earlier in this chapter). In becoming aware of our unconscious tendencies, we may hopefully moderate their more bizarre, negative effects. Furthermore, by raising the inferior function or attitude into consciousness, we may eventually learn to express their positive attributes. In this way the personality achieves a roundness or completeness that was not evident before.

The conscious recognition and differentiation of inferior tendencies is, however, a particularly difficult psychological task and one that Jung believed is best tackled only in the second half of life – generally speaking, after about the age of thirty-five. For most people, the more immediate concern should be consciously to differentiate the two potential auxiliary functions. Thus a person who is dominated by thinking should, in the interests of wholeness or completeness, begin to acknowledge and express either sensation or intuition (and eventually both). Yet it is important that this is attempted only after the dominant function has been clearly differentiated, otherwise confusion and disturbance will generally result.

Although in theory it should be possible to raise all four functions and both attitudes into consciousness, producing a fully 'rounded' individual, in practice the most that can usually be hoped is that the person learns to differentiate the dominant function and attitude, begins to express the two auxiliary functions, and becomes aware of the ways in which the inferior (unconscious) function and attitude are likely to manifest. Some progress towards this eventual goal may be made by studying the psychological type that is indicated in the Watchword matrix.

When considering psychological type it is important to bear in mind that while a mixed-function or ambivert matrix *may* be a sign of psychological maturity and the achievement of partial completeness, it can also indicate a failure to differentiate effectively the dominant function or attitude. In the absence of other evidence, it is usually impossible to determine which of these possibilities is the case, although with younger people it is perhaps more likely to be the latter. In the final analysis it is for each person to decide upon the significance of her or his own psychological typing.

6 The interpretive process

The depth and degree of elaboration of interpretation depends primarily upon the purpose you have in mind. If you have completed a matrix because you have a particular question or problem, then it will usually be necessary only to examine specific keys or to form a quick assessment of psychological type or of the overall flavour or theme of the matrix. If, on the other hand, you desire a complete psychological analysis, then interpretation will require a detailed consideration of all aspects of the matrix.

Interpretation is a skill that develops with practice. When you become more experienced you should be able to 'read' a matrix without the need to make lengthy notes and without referring continually to the key descriptions. Until the time, however, when you feel confident of your ability to analyse a matrix directly, it is recommended that interpretation is carried out systematically in the following stages.

STAGE 1: PSYCHOLOGICAL TYPE

As indicated in Chapter 5, an important basic consideration is the psychological type that is indicated in the matrix. This should be determined and evaluated using the procedures already described.

Psychological type has major implications for the further interpretation of a Watchword matrix. In general, interpretation will be found most straightforward when the matrix exhibits feeling or intuition because these two functions express more directly the truly *personal* dimension. In these cases, therefore, psychological themes may usually be identified fairly easily. In contrast, with matrices exhibiting thinking and, in particular, sensation the key words often seem rather superficial or dissociated from the personal domain.

Compare, for example, Matrices 39 and 40. Even without a detailed examination of each key it is clear that in the case of Matrix 40 (ambivert intuitive feeling) there is a strong psychological pattern of meanings involved. Matrix 39 (extraverted sensation or sensory feeling), however, probably appears at first sight to be almost devoid of any psychological significance.

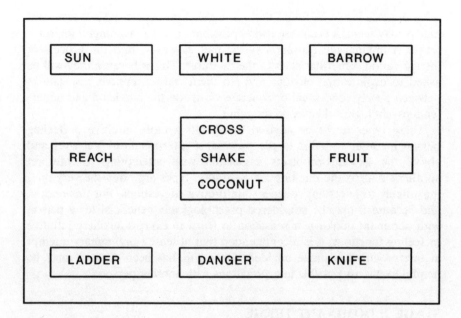

Matrix 39 (Rachel)

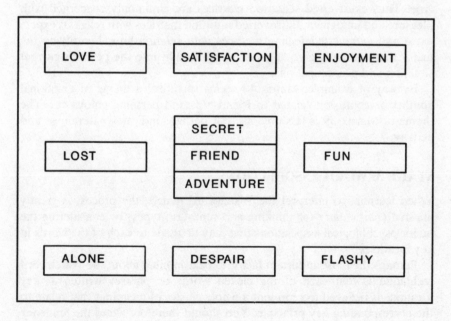

Matrix 40 (Jane)

In practice it will be found that no matter how superficial a Watchword matrix may seem, it is almost always possible to find a meaningful interpretation. Thinking and sensation types may, however, find the process of interpretation somewhat alien to their natures. This is because they will be asked to explore non-obvious and (to them) rather tenuous associations between purely conceptual or concrete words on the one hand and underlying psychological themes on the other.

These types might be advised to consult a more intuitive or feeling person in order to assist in the process of interpretation. Yet over and above the general problems associated with attempting to interpret another's matrix, the thinking and sensation types are often the very ones most likely to reject any 'deeper' interpretive suggestions. For this reason, and because it may be considered psychologically beneficial for a person with dominant thinking or sensation to learn to express auxiliary intuitive or feeling functions, it is recommended that at least a preliminary attempt at interpretation is made unaided. Once this has been done, it may be helpful to discuss possible interpretations with another person.

STAGE 2: DOMINANT THEME

Before examining each Watchword key in detail, it is often useful to consider the dominant theme (if any) that is expressed in the matrix. To a significant degree, these themes are generally consistent with psychological type. Thus extraverted sensation matrices are commonly concerned with pleasure and enjoyment, introverted intuition matrices with religious experience and extraverted feeling matrices with relationships. Identifying the major theme usually gives a good overall insight into the person's current situation and preoccupations.

By way of example, Matrix 40 seems to reflect a theme of emotional conflict or confusion related to friendships and personal enjoyment. The theme of Matrix 39 is less obvious, but perhaps indicates naturalness and activity.

STAGE 3: WORD ASSOCIATIONS

When learning to interpret the Watchword matrix, the process is greatly assisted (particularly for thinking and sensation types) by considering the major psychological associations that may be made to each of the words in key locations.

Perhaps the most important factor to bear in mind about the Watchword technique is that each of the eleven words or phrases written at key locations is believed to represent a whole cluster of meanings that relate to the corresponding key principle. You should therefore avoid the tendency to consider a word only on the basis of its most salient or literal interpretation. Instead you must allow each word to suggest or hint at a complex of subtle and interconnected meanings, any one or any combination of which may provide the basis for interpretation.

The method of association that should be used is the Jungian technique of *amplification* in which the meaning of an idea is elaborated by forming a number of associations each of which is directly and immediately connected to the original image (see, for example, Jacobi, 1968; Jung, 1968c, 1977). For example, the meaning of 'fur' might be amplified by considering these associations: fur – cat, fur – soft, fur – warm, fur – expensive. With Jungian amplification it is important at each stage to return to the original concept. This method is to be distinguished from the Freudian technique of *free association* in which a chain of connected images is formed by allowing one idea to lead to another, which in turn leads to another, and so on. Freudian free association might therefore produce the following sequence: fur – cat – milk – breast – mother – hate. While it is true that this technique may lead eventually to some underlying psychological obstruction or complex, the final endpoint will usually bear little relationship to the original idea. For this reason, the Freudian technique cannot be applied to the Watchword matrix.

Jungian amplification allows not only personal associations but also cultural and universal or archetypal links. For example on a personal level you might associate 'cow' with stupidity or bitchiness. Culturally, however, 'cow' is associated with food and farming, while archetypally it represents the earth, spiritual nourishment and the maternal principle. Although personal associations should be given primary consideration, it can also be

Table 6 Examples of word associations

'Haze'	'Biscuits'	'Rain'
Uncertainty	Pleasure	Unhappy
Lack of clarity	Temptation	Weeping
Blindness	Crumbling	Wet
Confusion	Sweetness	Cold
Unconscious	Relaxation	Dismal
Future	Break	Refreshed
Mysterious	Insubstantial	Rebirth

'Catch'	'Diary'	'Patient'
Problem	Sense of identity	Waiting
Difficulty	Self-awareness	Illness
Sexual conquest	Past	Dependence
Attraction	Personal secrets	Vulnerability
Possession	Intimacy	Recuperation
Holding tight	Memories	Undemanding
Pursuit	Organized	Caring

useful to explore both cultural and archetypal dimensions. In this respect it may be found helpful to ask others what they associate with certain images or to consult books on mythology and symbolism.

It is often worthwhile, especially with early attempts at interpretation, to write down a list of all the things that you can associate with each of the words in key locations. In particular, try to concentrate on features that have clear psychological significance. Do not censor your thoughts in any way, or attempt to ensure that all the associations are mutually consistent. When the word you are considering is a concrete object that has no obvious psychological associations, it is sometimes helpful to focus upon its various physical properties (e.g., hard vs soft, rough vs smooth, heavy vs light) since these will generally have psychological connotations.

Some examples of this associative process are shown in Table 6. Note that at this stage ambiguous words should be allowed to suggest alternative meanings (e.g., 'patient' can refer to both illness and waiting).

STAGE 4: KEY INTERPRETATIONS

It is recommended that each of the Watchword keys is interpreted separately before any attempt is made to interrelate the meanings of the various keys or to examine dynamic processes within the matrix. Notes of possible meanings that may be attributed to each key should be made by relating the word you have written in the location (together with its major amplifications) to the detailed description of the key given in Chapter 4.

It may also be useful to assess the psychological function (sensation, intuition, thinking or feeling) that is expressed by each key. This is because, with mixed types, different functions are sometimes found in different areas of the matrix. Alternatively, even with predominantly single-function matrices, one or two atypical functions may be indicated at specific key locations. In the case of ambivert matrices also, different attitudes (introversion or extraversion) are commonly exhibited in different areas. In practice, all of these features can be of considerable interpretive significance.

The suggested order in which the keys should be examined is as follows:

1 *Giant*
2 *Dwarf*
3 *Soul*
4 *Persona*
5 *Guide*
6 *Imago*
7 *Shadow*
8 *Spectre*
9 *Station*
10 *Battle*
11 *Destiny*

As an example of key interpretation, Table 7 summarizes possible meanings for Matrix 39 (Rachel).

Having completed this stage, you should have a fairly clear idea of whether or not the Watchword technique has 'worked' for you and should be able to place at least a provisional interpretation upon most, if not all, of the Watchword keys. Generally you should feel that, taken together, the keys are capable of forming the basis of a coherent narrative account of your present situation or personality.

If you have difficulty interpreting a particular key then an examination of the two words that were associated to form it may help to establish its underlying meaning. In cases of major difficulty it may be necessary to think of another linking word or phrase and then to interpret this alternative link. If a change is made to a key word, however, it is not recommended that other (later) key words are altered, even though these were derived from a sequence of associations that was based upon the original word.

To clarify and develop interpretation, important internal relationships between keys should next be examined. Two distinct kinds of internal relationships exist within the Watchword matrix. These are (a) dialectical relationships and (b) developmental relationships.

STAGE 5: DIALECTICAL RELATIONSHIPS

Dialectical relationships reflect the manner in which the Watchword matrix is constructed. Thus each key word may be viewed as a resolution, or synthesis, of two opposing ideas.

The seven dialectical relationships inherent in the Watchword matrix are shown in Table 8. In each case the words you have written in the three related locations should be examined (together with their major associations) in an attempt to understand (a) the nature of the opposition or contradiction involved between poles and (b) the sense in which the synthesizing word provides a meaningful resolution of this conflict.

As an example of the way in which dialectical relationships may be interpreted, consider Rachel's *Guide – Shadow – Soul* trio (Matrix 39). The opposition that is implied here seems to be between an untroubled, innocent, lazy enjoyment of life (represented by 'sun') and the need to strive hard and long in order to climb towards success or happiness (represented by 'ladder'). Since these words are in the *Guide* and *Shadow* locations, respectively, they probably indicate that, whereas Rachel's deepest inner yearnings are for an easy, relaxed life of pleasure, there may be an unwillingness to accept fully the strong personal need for success and social advancement, or the necessity of hard, sustained effort. In practice, Rachel may be lazy or too 'laid back' and may expect happiness or success to come easily, on a plate.

Table 7 Key interpretations for Matrix 39 (Rachel)

Key	Word (Function)	Major associations	Possible meanings
Giant	White (S)	Bright Clean Pure Virginal Clarity	Fundamental drives or virtues = spiritual or physical purity, intellectual clarity, or innocence.
Dwarf	Danger (NF)	Difficulty Threat Risk Insecurity Fear	Feelings of insecurity or fear are causing restriction or stagnation. Sense of peril, threat or major difficulty.
Soul	Reach (N)	Striving Deficiency Need Achievement Success Ambition Frustration	Failure fully to acknowledge or realize inner personality or emotions. Feelings of dissatisfaction or emptiness. Possibly attracted to men who are ambitious or successful.
Persona	Fruit (S)	Growth Ripeness Maturity Completion Birth Comical Productive	Witty or comical character? Ripening or maturing of the outer personality or of social roles. Fairly comfortable and productive material existence.
Guide	Sun (S)	Happiness Warmth Relaxation Openness Perfection Clarity Light	Deep inner yearning for happiness, comfort and relaxation, for personal perfection, for clear awareness or for knowledge.
Imago	Barrow (S)	Selling Market place Gardening Earth Harvest	Attracted to career in sales, trading, agriculture, or gardening? Ideal self = earthy, natural, nature-loving.
Shadow	Ladder (S)	Climbing Striving Effort Status Success Opportunity	Unrecognized or unconscious need for success or social advancement. An unconsciously motivated social climber? May project these tendencies onto others. Unrecognized opportunities?
Spectre	Knife	Pain Violence	Fear of pain, violence or death. Dread of becoming violent

	(SF)	Killing Cutting Sharpness	or vicious. A sharp or cutting nature that may cause personal difficulties?
Station	Coconut (S)	Hard shell Rough Sweetness Milk White flesh Nourishment Sexuality	Basic sense of self = rough or hard exterior but also strong maternal or nurturing tendencies. Natural sweetness. Feminine sexuality.
Battle	Cross (SF)	Anger Problem Conflict Choice Religion	Need for major choice or decision to be made. Important conflict or problem that self must resolve (perhaps related to religion or to feelings of anger).
Destiny	Shake (SF)	Shake-up Change Anger Threaten Anxiety	Major shake-up or change in personal life seems inevitable. This change may be highly threatening or anxiety provoking, or may involve the expression of anger.

The resolution of this opposition is represented by 'reach' in the *Soul* (animus) location. This may indicate that Rachel is strongly attracted to men who achieve something with their lives. More importantly it suggests an inner awareness (although perhaps not consciously acknowledged) that personal success and happiness have yet to be realized, but need to be worked towards. Perhaps also (since 'reach' is essentially intuitive) it indicates that Rachel needs to look beyond superficial, purely sensual pleasures, to the fulfilment of some deeper purpose.

Another interesting example is provided by Jane's *Shadow – Spectre – Dwarf* trio (Matrix 40). The opposition here seems to be between (a)

Table 8 The seven dialectical relationships

Opposing poles				Resolution
Guide	vs	*Shadow*	=	*Soul*
Imago	vs	*Spectre*	=	*Persona*
Guide	vs	*Imago*	=	*Giant*
Shadow	vs	*Spectre*	=	*Dwarf*
Soul	vs	*Persona*	=	*Station*
Giant	vs	*Dwarf*	=	*Battle*
Station	vs	*Battle*	=	*Destiny*

insularity, noninvolvement or unsociability (represented by 'alone') and (b) ostentatious showiness or swanky extraversion (represented by 'flashy'). Since 'flashy' is in the *Spectre* location, this suggests that Jane may recognize in the self or other people (yet fundamentally dislikes or disapproves of) a tendency towards ostentation and a flaunting of the personality. At the same time, 'alone' in the *Shadow* location indicates that insular, unsociable characteristics may be repressed or held in check. The tension that is generated by a rejection of extraverted qualities and a simultaneous failure to accept or express more introverted traits seems to produce in Jane something of a psychological impasse. Thus the resolution of these opposites is represented by 'despair' in the *Dwarf* location. This indicates that feelings of hopelessness and dejection may tend to overpower Jane because of her inability to differentiate or come to terms with the introverted and extraverted sides of her own nature (it may be noted that this matrix is clearly ambivert).

STAGE 6: DEVELOPMENTAL RELATIONSHIPS

In addition to the dialectical relationships discussed in the previous section, the structure of the Watchword matrix identifies certain major developmental processes within the psyche. An understanding of developmental relationships is particularly important because it can help the individual to establish the major area or areas of life where change is taking place. Also it may give some indication of the next step forward.

There are three developmental sequences inherent in the Watchword matrix. These are summarized in Figure 13.

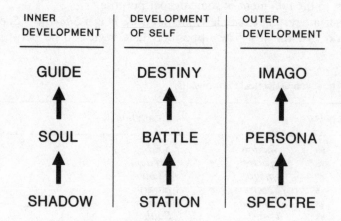

Figure 13 The three developmental relationships

Outer development

Outer development refers to those processes that lead the person to success, happiness and fulfilment in the material or social worlds. Development generally starts from a position of weakness, alienation, anxiety or difficulty (represented by *Spectre*). Through the achievement of a stable outer personality and by adopting appropriate social roles (*Persona*), the individual may eventually approach his or her consciously realized goals (*Imago*).

Inner development

Inner development is a much more subtle process, represented by the sequence *Shadow – Soul – Guide.* This sequence involves a journey towards deeper knowledge of the inner workings of the psyche. Significantly, the sequence implied in the Watchword matrix is identical with that suggested by Jung in his outline of the process of *individuation* (see, for example, Jacobi, 1968; Jung, 1966, 1968b; von Franz, 1964). Thus Jung argues that individuation involves successive stages or milestones of development in which the person encounters archetypal images of (a) the *shadow*, (b) the *soul-image* (anima or animus) and (c) the *mana personality*, or archetype of power. According to Jung these three stages of development must precede the final realization of the archetype of the *self.*

In simple terms, for inner development to occur, we must first of all confront the dark, hidden, undifferentiated or repressed side of our nature (the shadow). An important aspect of this is the person's inferior attitude and function type. Coming to terms with our personal shadow involves a willingness to assess ourselves critically and ruthlessly and to accept the darkness that we find as an essential part of our own being, rather than as a fault in others.

At the second stage we must encounter our complementary, contra-sexual aspect. Thus the male must be willing to accept his own inner femininity (the anima) rather than attempt to achieve completion by searching for such qualities in women. Similarly, females must accept their inner masculinity (the animus) instead of looking for these complementary characteristics in their men. Essentially we must realize that our yearning for completion (although symbolized in sexual terms) comes from within our own psyche and therefore cannot be fully satisfied by another. This does not mean, of course, that we cannot or need not relate meaningfully with members of the opposite sex. What it does mean, however, is that we should learn to relate to them as the individual whole *persons* that they are, and not as symbols of our own completion or as satisfiers of our own psychological needs.

The third stage in the individuation process involves the confrontation with our deepest, most powerful yearnings, or our mana personality. As we have seen (Chapter 4) these most basic tendencies are, Jung believed, different for men and women. In realizing the source and nature of our own inner power (e.g., our essential maleness or femaleness) we must, however, avoid the temptation to identify with this powerful image, thereby falling into the trap of spiritual pride, self-importance or megalomania.

Two stages of life?

Jung suggests that the development of the outer personality precedes (or should precede) the archetypal inner process of individuation (e.g., Jacobi, 1968; Jung, 1969). Thus he argues that outer development, or the *initiation into outward reality*, should be the task of the first half of life (until about 35 years of age). Only in the second half, perhaps following a mid-life crisis, should inner development, or *initiation into inner reality*, become a major concern.

Although some critics and neo-Jungians have disputed the idea that outer and inner development can be so conveniently identified as tasks of the first and second halves of life (see, for example, Samuels, 1985) Jung's suggestion is useful in pointing to the dangers of becoming carried away with analysing deep inner processes when more pressing concerns may revolve around social or material needs. On the other hand, the theory also identifies the mistake made by those who remain tied to the outer domain and who fail to consider the need for inner development.

In practice it is important to allow a certain flexibility in Jung's proposal. In the first place it must be recognized that the personal 'crisis' that may serve to divide the two halves of life does not occur universally in the mid-thirties; there is great individual variation. People who have established a fairly stable material existence, and who feel reasonably comfortable with the public self, would therefore be foolish to deny a valid interest in the inner processes of individuation simply because they are theoretically under-age.

More importantly, it is probably a mistake to believe that the transition between outer and inner development is so sudden and irrevocable. Many people, it would seem, find it not only possible but also necessary to develop simultaneously on both fronts, although the relative priorities given to inner and outer development may not always be equal. In general terms, Jung is certainly right in arguing that a concern with outer development is usually associated with youth, whereas inner development tends to dominate the later years. Yet changes in personal circumstances such as unemployment, divorce or illness might well require an older person to forsake a current preoccupation with inner development in order to tackle once again the problems of coping with the outer world.

In the context of this discussion, it is important to note that the processes of inner and outer development should not be confused with the psychological attitudes of introversion and extraversion. Thus an introverted attitude does not necessarily imply that inner development takes priority, neither does extraversion implicate outer development. Young introverts have to learn to adapt to outer reality, while mature extraverts should ideally begin to consider the inner dimension. On the other hand an introverted attitude is certainly more compatible with the inner process of individuation, whereas extraversion is more consistent with adaptation to the physical and social worlds. According to Jung this generally means that extraverts have a rather easier time in the first half of life, while introverts are relatively better fitted for the tasks of the second half.

Although either inner or outer development may be uppermost at any particular time, the Watchword technique is based on the assumption that both processes are potentially available to the psyche and are reflected in the left (inner) and right (outer) sides of the matrix. By studying each side we may therefore be assisted in the important task of learning to differentiate these two processes within our own being. More than this, in order to achieve true psychological wholeness we must acknowledge, I believe, our continuing need for both inner and outer development. At some level of our being these two processes are ever active and both are always necessary. Ideally, and irrespective of which process may currently seem to be dominant, each person should therefore attempt to learn from the messages contained in both sides of the matrix.

Development of self

The achievement in some measure of both outer and inner development paves the way for the *development of the self*, represented in the Watchword matrix by the sequence *Station – Battle – Destiny*. In being formed from the conjunction of *Soul* and *Persona*, *Station* always expresses some kind of perceived balance or tension between the inner and outer dimensions of our experience. *Station* thus indicates our personal axis, our fixed centre or *static self*. In practice it generally reflects our present understanding of 'where we are at', or our sense of basic identity. Essentially, therefore, it denotes the individual's typical response to the questions 'Who am I?' or 'Where am I?'

Station is not our final destination. Rather it is the starting point for the self's journey along the path towards full realization. Development of the self cannot take place without change or movement, yet the primary obstacle to such development often lies in our own inertia and resistance to change. Our sense of identity is so important to us that any anticipated alteration in the self may be viewed as a threat to our basic existence and therefore as something to be avoided. In this way we may cling to the familiar and may be unwilling to step forward into the world of unknown possibilities. At other times it might seem that external forces or conditions are preventing us from developing towards self-realization. Perhaps we see ourselves as constrained by poverty, inadequate education, lack of opportunities or the domineering influence of friends or family.

The most important thing to recognize about development of the self is that it almost always takes place against a backdrop of conflict and opposition. Contrary to certain opinion, self-realization is rarely if ever a free-wheeling joy-ride towards perfection. Rather it is a continual uphill struggle against obstacles and barriers of our own as well as others' making.

The nature of our personal struggle is represented in the Watchword matrix by *Battle*, a symbol of the *dynamic self*, or the self in motion. Examining the theme of the word at this location should give some idea of the fundamental direction in which the self needs to move, or the major personal obstacles that need to be overcome.

The projected outcome of the self's battle or quest is represented by *Destiny*, itself a symbol of the *realized self*. *Destiny* generally reveals something of our ideal state of being, of the person we might become when all oppositions, tensions and conflicts in the psyche are resolved. Its meaning should be studied deeply and carefully for, in an important sense, this key indicates the light that we carry before us. *Destiny* is the final distillation of the whole Watchword matrix and we should constantly remind ourselves of its significance as we continue with our everyday preoccupations and struggles. Thus *Destiny* may almost be considered as a kind of personal touchstone against which we may evaluate our current motivations and life experiences.

Of course, sometimes *Destiny* does not indicate an ideal with which we would wish to be associated. At such times the key may communicate an important message about the direction our life is taking, or will take, unless we do something to avoid the consequences. As indicated earlier, there is nothing inevitable about any part of the Watchword matrix, and the individual must not be afraid to challenge his or her 'destiny' when this seems appropriate or desirable.

Comparison of Watchword and Jung

Before considering an example of the interpretation of developmental relationships, it is interesting to compare in more detail the model of personal development implied in the Watchword matrix with that suggested by Carl Jung. The assumption behind the Watchword technique is essentially that the three developmental processes (i.e., outer development, inner development and development of self) are all represented in the matrix and therefore that it is possible, at the present time, to obtain at least a partial knowledge of each. This does not mean that the necessary work has to be, or can be, carried out simultaneously on every front. As we have seen, either inner or outer development may dominate current experience. It may also be that a particular developmental achievement is necessary in one of these areas before any further progress can be made in the other. Development of self, however, must inevitably lag behind outer and inner development since it depends upon the integration of these two processes.

In its basics, this model is remarkably similar to that put forward by Jung. One difference, already considered, is that Jung implied that outer development must precede the inner process of individuation. Watchword, on the other hand, allows both processes to be acknowledged and worked upon at the same time. Furthermore, Jung suggests that the realization of the archetype of the *self* is the final stage in the individuation process, taking place after the confrontation with the mana personality and involving the meaningful unification of all aspects and opposites within the

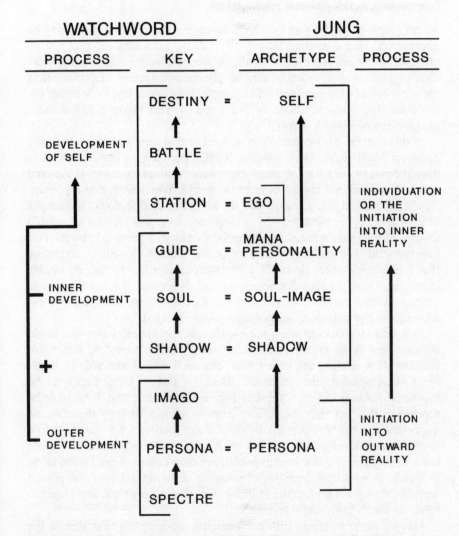

Figure 14 Comparison of the developmental models of Watchword and Jung

psyche. Watchword differs in this respect primarily in proposing a separate developmental sequence for the process of self-realization. This sequence incorporates movement of the self from a basically static concept of identity (*Station*, or the Jungian *ego*), through dynamic confrontations with moral, spiritual or existential conflicts (*Battle*), to the achievement of a final integrated resolution (*Destiny*, or the Jungian *realized self*).

To aid this comparison of the two models, Figure 14 summarizes the suggested parallels and differences between Jungian concepts and processes and those implied by the structure of the Watchword matrix.

Interpreting developmental relationships

As an example of the way in which developmental relationships may be interpreted, Jane's matrix (Matrix 40) will be examined. In this matrix, outer development is indicated by the sequence 'flashy – fun – enjoyment'. This suggests that in order to achieve greater satisfaction or fulfilment in the outer world of objects and other people, Jane needs first to confront the anxieties that seem to relate to her concern with being exhibitionistic, exaggerated or vain (*Spectre*).

In this context it is interesting to remember that Jane's matrix is basically ambivert, itself suggesting a possible conflict between an introverted with-drawal from or rejection of outer expression, and an extraverted demand for total, uninhibited involvement in the world. With this in mind, perhaps Jane's introverted side requires that she moderates exhibitionist tendencies or learns to express what may be seen as the more positive and acceptable aspects of her extraversion such as gaiety, vitality or personal charm. This interpretation is consistent with 'fun' in the *Persona* location, suggesting that Jane's basic outer personality is vivacious and fun-loving. By openly expressing these positive characteristics and by limiting the more negative, outrageous and excessive manifestations of extraversion, Jane may eventually achieve her conscious goal of enjoyment (*Imago*).

Jane was 19 years old when the matrix was completed, a fact that might indicate that these processes of outer development should be her major concern. However, to the extent that Jane feels willing and able to tackle inner development, the sequence 'alone – lost – love' needs to be examined. 'Alone' in the *Shadow* location indicates that Jane may be repressing the fact that she suffers from loneliness. It may therefore be important for her to open up to these deep feelings of isolation before further inner development can occur. Alternatively, perhaps Jane should learn to recognize, and accept as part of her own nature, a need to be alone at times, to withdraw from social contact, or to retreat into the private world of thoughts and fantasies (once again, this is a problem that seems to relate to Jane's basic ambiversion).

Having come to terms with her personal shadow, the next step in the process of inner development is for Jane to confront her soul-image, represented by 'lost' (*Soul*). In Jungian terms this is believed to represent an aspect of Jane's animus, her inner male counterpart. The chosen word is particularly interesting and may indicate confusion about the 'masculine' side of her nature. Perhaps Jane feels uncomfortable or out of her depth when expressing what may seem to her to be 'mannish' characteristics such as arrogance, argumentativeness or intellectualism. This in turn may lead her to seek completion by attempting to find such qualities in male part-ners. Or it may be that 'lost' indicates a vulnerable, innocent, childlike inner nature that, if unrecognized, may result in Jane being attracted to men who are weak, ingenuous, sexually inexperienced or boyish.

In learning to recognize these possible animus projections, the way is open for Jane to confront her mana personality, represented by 'love' in the *Guide* location. This key may indicate that Jane's deepest inner yearn-ings are for love, care and protection. On the other hand it might also suggest that the source of Jane's true inner power is her own ability to love, care and protect. Interestingly this latter interpretation would be consistent with Jung's belief that, for women, the mana personality typically takes the form of the Great Earth Mother.

Once work has begun on the outer and inner dimensions of personal development, Jane may then address the problem of self development, represented by the sequence 'adventure – secret – friend'. 'Adventure' in the *Station* location suggests either that Jane possesses a basically adventu-rous spirit, or that she sees her current situation as being exciting and as presenting great opportunities for the self. In this respect it is pertinent to note that Jane completed the matrix only a few weeks after beginning a full-time degree course.

'Secret' in the *Battle* location may seem difficult to interpret until it is realized that the word has been formed from the resolution of 'satisfaction' and 'despair'. It appears, therefore, that Jane's main obstacle to self-devel-opment may be a tendency to keep important emotions veiled and unex-pressed. In order to progress she may need to open up emotionally and allow others to penetrate her private world of feelings. This may then enable Jane to form the kind of significant friendships that she seems ulti-mately to value (i.e., *Destiny* = 'friend').

It is interesting to note how many of the developmental problems expe-rienced by Jane seem to be a consequence or expression of her ambiverted attitude. Because Jane is quite young it would appear that her ambiversion may reflect a failure to differentiate her dominant conscious attitude rather than a mature integration of introversion and extraversion. The matrix therefore indicates that this is an area needing particular attention.

STAGE 7: SYNTHESIZING THE MATRIX

The final task in the interpretation of a Watchword matrix is to attempt a meaningful integration or synthesis of the various tendencies, forces, conflicts and processes that have been identified in the previous stages. Important themes should be brought out clearly and apparent contradictions should be given careful consideration as these often reveal subtle complexities in our personal situation or psychological make-up. The main purpose of this integration should be to paint a self-portrait that is not only recognizable but also personally helpful. In the final analysis if you cannot extract practical lessons from the Watchword technique then it becomes little more than an idle, if amusing, pastime.

You may find it useful, particularly with early attempts at interpretation, to write a descriptive summary of the matrix in the form of a detailed psychological report, such as might be prepared for a client. This procedure will help you to focus on the major indications and will encourage you to organize and integrate these into a coherent and readable narrative account. You should end with a few important conclusions, especially concerning the way forward.

7 An example of self-analysis

Watchword is essentially a method of *self*-analysis in which it is important for individuals to form their own interpretive assessments. This is mainly because only the person who has completed the matrix knows the full facts of his or her situation. Furthermore, the words chosen for the various key locations will often have very personal or private significance that will not be apparent to someone else. Self-analysis also removes the possibility that another person might, consciously or unconsciously, manipulate the interpretation of your matrix for some ulterior purpose. Of course we can always deceive ourselves during interpretation, but this is generally much less hazardous than allowing unqualified others to interfere with the intimate process of self-examination.

If you have friends whose opinions and impartiality you can trust, then you may find it helpful to discuss your interpretations with them. If nothing else, talking to another person about your matrix will encourage you to formulate your ideas clearly and to probe more deeply into the self. In this context, it is worth repeating that the Watchword matrix may also provide a most effective focus for counselling or psychotherapy. You should be wary, however, of allowing others (even if professionally qualified as counsellors or therapists) to impose interpretations, although any suggestions they offer should be given due consideration.

To show in some detail how the Watchword technique may be used to provide a basis for self-analysis I have decided, for the reasons discussed, to present an example matrix of my own rather than to report at secondhand another's experience. This decision is made somewhat reluctantly, partly because of doubts that might be raised about the objectivity of my interpretation and partly out of a natural sense of privacy. On balance, however, this seems the most sensible course.

The matrix I shall consider (Matrix 41) is the one I first completed under the direction of my colleague in 1984. At this time the Watchword system had yet to be formulated and I was unaware of the purpose of the exercise I was carrying out. Additional associations were made several months later once the structural principles of the Watchword matrix were established. To aid interpretation, the matrix includes the eight words immediately

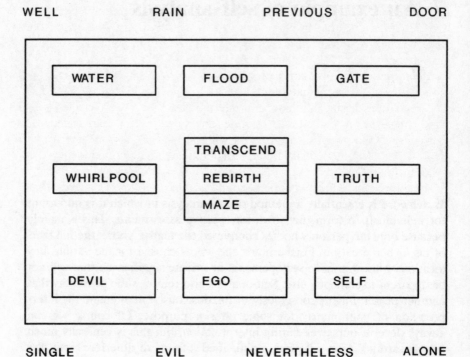

WELL   RAIN   PREVIOUS   DOOR

| WATER | FLOOD | GATE |

| WHIRLPOOL | TRANSCEND / REBIRTH / MAZE | TRUTH |

| DEVIL | EGO | SELF |

SINGLE   EVIL   NEVERTHELESS   ALONE

Matrix 41 (Author)

outside the main rectangle so that the derivation of all key words may be seen.

A few relevant facts about my personal situation in 1984 will help to place the matrix in context. I was 34 years old. Five months before completing the exercise my wife and I had separated after ten years together. We had no children and I was now living alone in our marital home. Most of my energies became directed into my work as a polytechnic lecturer, into academic research and into hobbies and rather solitary interests. I had no family living in the area and few close friends. My main emotional concern at the time was a feeling that I had 'blown' my marriage and would probably need to wait a considerable period of time before I was able to develop another close romantic involvement.

STAGE 1: PSYCHOLOGICAL TYPE

The matrix is a good example of a seemingly pure introverted intuition type. Several of the key words clearly reflect an awareness of deep inner processes ('transcend', 'rebirth', 'truth', 'ego', 'self') while the other words are strongly archetypal in their symbolism ('water', 'flood', 'gate', 'whirlpool', 'maze', 'devil') therefore indicating introverted intuition rather than introverted sensation. The description of the introverted intuitive type (see Chapter 5) is one that in many ways I can identify with. In a sense this book is itself testimony to a certain visionary or, some might say, cranky imagination.

Being unmixed, the matrix suggests that I have probably succeeded in one of the major tasks that Jung allocates to the first half of life, i.e., the differentiation of the dominant attitude and function type. At the same time, however, it indicates a definite one-sidedness or narrowness of perspective. An important future task will therefore be for me to learn to express one or both auxiliary functions (thinking and feeling) as well as the other attitude type (extraversion). Even though it is not directly indicated in the matrix, my educational background and academic work suggest that thinking is likely to present the least problem. The conscious expression of feeling and extraversion, on the other hand, may be much more difficult.

Because consciousness is dominated by introversion and intuition, this implies that extraversion and sensation will tend to be unconscious and inferior, expressing themselves in primitive or infantile ways. Certainly I recognize that an immaturity, gaucheness or childishness often characterizes my attempts to be sociable. Given the choice, for example, I would much prefer to play party games or demonstrate magic tricks than make 'adult' conversation. Repression of sensation is indicated in several ways. Thus I am inclined to neglect physical needs such as those for food and clothing. My tastes are simple and I am generally untidy and rather ascetic by nature. I become easily bored when on holiday or away from work and hobbies. At the same time I can be compulsive or obsessive about personal hygiene or safety, about collecting, about neatness of work or about the general routines of daily life.

STAGE 2: DOMINANT THEME

It is hard to identify a single dominant theme in this matrix. In general, however, the matrix seems to reflect a need to overcome or transcend archetypal conflicts between good and evil, order and anarchy, safety and danger, or inhibition and involvement. The matrix therefore indicates a time of major personal crisis that focuses upon the moral, spiritual or existential implications of current difficulties.

This is consistent with the situation I found myself in, relating in particular to the break-up of my marriage. Thus I was preoccupied with worries about the personal consequences of separation, about my adequacy in relationships, about the uncertainty of my future and generally about what I ought to do now with my life. In many ways I viewed my situation as one in which I was being 'tested' by life or fate. To pass this personal examination I would need to resolve not simply the natural but essentially temporary emotional reactions to separation but also more fundamental questions of where I stood and what I stood for. In this respect it is

Table 9 Stage 3: Word associations (Author, 1984)

Key	Word (Function)	Major associations
Giant	Flood (N)	Catharsis. Overcome with emotions. Destruction. New Life. Dissemination. Involvement. Increase. Abundance. 'Go forth and multiply.' Spiritual influx. Initiation. Baptism.
Dwarf	Ego (N)	Egocentrism. Small-mindedness. Selfishness. Lack of concern for others. Personal desire and craving. Spiritual failure. Obstacle to enlightenment.
Soul	Whirlpool (N)	Confusion. Out of control. Lost. Powerful force. 'Drag me down.' Danger. Magnetic attraction.
Persona	Truth (N)	Honest. Trustworthy. Open. Lack of duplicity. Reliable. Accurate. Innocent. Intellectual. Intelligent. Wise.
Guide	Water (N)	Emotional. Sensitive. Receptive. Yielding. Fluidity. Spontaneity. Spirituality. Romanticism. Naturalness. Intuitive.
Imago	Gate (N)	Opening. Opportunities. Control. Invitation. Exclusion. Barrier. Outside. Sexual experience.
Shadow	Devil (N)	Personal wickedness. Evil. Domination. Violence. Cruelty. Anger. Exploitation. Degeneracy. Lust. Materialism. Darkness.
Spectre	Self (N)	Loneliness. Lack of relationships. Self-reliance. Solitude. Self-preoccupation.
Station	Maze (N)	Quest. Hero. Searching. Lost. Self-discovery. Confusion. Difficulty. Identity crisis.
Battle	Transcend (N)	Transcendence of self. Overcome problems. Spiritual progress. Enlightenment. Larger perspective. Expand horizons.
Destiny	Rebirth (N)	Spiritual initiation. New start. Reawakening. Healing. Making whole. Fresh vitality.

interesting to note that I completed this matrix almost exactly at Jung's theoretical midpoint of life.

STAGE 3: WORD ASSOCIATIONS

Table 9 presents the major associations (amplifications) that I have formed to each of the key words.

STAGE 4: KEY INTERPRETATIONS

Giant = 'flood'

I remember clearly that this key seemed particularly significant at the time. For me, 'flood' carried strong spiritual or archetypal overtones, especially so as it was a word I had derived from the highly symbolic combination of 'water–gate'. This indicated to me the importance of opening up to an influx of spiritual energies at a time when my personal and emotional life was at such a low ebb. I felt that the moment was one of great spiritual opportunity and that I should allow myself to be swept along on a tide that was not of my own making but that represented something 'beyond' that was strong and good.

There was another sense in which 'flood' was significant. This related directly to my personal situation and carried implications about opening up the emotional 'flood-gates'. Certainly in many ways the break-up of my marriage had apparently affected me much less than I might have anticipated. An outside observer probably would have thought I was coping well in the circumstances and that I had managed to come through the trauma emotionally unscathed. For much of the time this was also my own consciously held view. Yet the reality of the situation was that I had failed to acknowledge or experience fully the pain of separation. In attempting, in classical fashion, to defend myself psychologically by blocking out these powerful feelings I was stifling all emotional expression. I was also denying myself the opportunity of a true coming to terms with my situation.

'Flood' in the *Giant* location points clearly to the need for some kind of emotional catharsis. The key seems to be urging me to drop my defences, to open up and own up to the feelings I was repressing. Only by allowing the flood of emotions to overwhelm me could the process of healing take its natural course.

Dwarf = 'ego'

This key suggests to me that development was being inhibited by an over-concern with protecting my own self-esteem and by a narrow-minded, self-orientated approach to life that failed to take a genuine interest in other people.

In relation to my personal situation, the key seems to be referring primarily to the ego defences that I was adopting in order to avoid the full emotional impact of my recent separation. In seeking to maintain the illusion that 'I' was coping and in control, my ego was preventing any genuine realization of my predicament and thereby obstructing any healing or growth. 'Ego' also signals a tendency to take myself too seriously, to become cloistered in my own shell, and to see things only from an ego-centric viewpoint. This in turn suggests the need to go out from the self to form meaningful relationships with others.

Soul = 'whirlpool'

To the extent that *Soul* represents the private, inner world of feelings, then 'whirlpool' was a particularly apt symbol at the time. Emotionally my life was in turmoil even though I may not have allowed myself to experience this fully. Inwardly I was confused, lost, at the mercy of powerful emotions that I hardly recognized and could not understand but that threatened to drag me down and out of control. The few clumsy attempts I had made in the previous months to start up new romantic involvements had ended in disappointment and served only to exacerbate my condition. As a result, perhaps I began to feel that the women to whom I was attracted were turbulent and unpredictable, even dangerous, and thus the principal source of my problems.

This projection of what was my own emotional situation onto members of the opposite sex is a classical expression of the Jungian anima. In being aware of this possibility I was fortunately able in some measure to recognize the process in my own being and thus maybe I was spared some of its more excessive or bizarre consequences. In spite of this, my relationships with women since this time have sometimes been stormy and confused. It would seem, therefore, that this is an area of my life that particularly needs to be worked upon.

Persona = 'truth'

'Truth' provides an interesting symbol of my outer personality, or public self. In many respects I probably initially appear to others as a rather intelligent, quiet, honest and reliable person. This public image generally fits fairly comfortably. It is a mask that I wear so naturally that perhaps it may seem not to be a mask at all, but my own 'true nature'. Yet one important message that the Watchword matrix delivers is that, like the other keys, *Persona* is only one aspect of our total being and therefore is not something to be identified with. Nevertheless, because I feel reasonably happy with my outer persona and because it represents a style of behaviour that in practice works quite well in my social and professional life, then there does not appear to be any great need for change in this area. On the other hand it is important, if for no other purpose than greater self-understanding, always to be aware that one's public image may be a relatively superficial pose that does not necessarily represent anything deep or enduring, and that may contradict other elements in one's make-up.

This key also suggests that 'truth' is, or was, a dominant conscious concern. There is without doubt in my character an important measure both of intellectual curiosity and a deeper philosophical or spiritual searching. At the same time I enjoy work that requires precision and a meticulous attention to detail. In this sense there seems to be a part of me that insists on having things 'right' and 'true'. Thus I detest dishonesty, falsehood, hypocrisy, negligence, ignorance and inaccuracy, whether in myself or in others. Although, considered favourably, these tendencies may simply reflect a love of truth, I recognize also that they easily turn into impatience, stuffiness, pedantry or intolerance. Perhaps, therefore, there is a warning inherent in this key that 'truth' could become a personal obsession. Also, because this word appears in the *Persona* location, I am forced to question whether my avowed concern with intellectual matters, authenticity or truth may in fact be a posture or act that I put on in order to impress others rather than because it is something fundamental to my nature.

Guide = 'water'

'Water' is, for me, primarily a symbol of natural spontaneity, emotional responsiveness, romantic idealism and spiritual insight. These meanings are remarkably consistent with the *Guide* principle. The key suggests that my particular inner strength, my mana personality, the source of any personal fascination I might possess, is a certain innocence, sensitivity or idealistic fervour. At the same time it may point to an instinctual leaning towards spiritual concerns.

In terms of any 'message' that this key may communicate, I seem to be being urged to relax emotionally and to yield to the natural course of events that my life needs to take. Furthermore, the key may be encouraging me to take a more idealistic, spiritual or philosophical perspective on my current situation; perhaps to focus rather less on short-term, personal difficulties and rather more on developing spiritual awareness.

Imago = 'gate'

The meaning of 'gate' seems to focus primarily upon its function as a mechanism for allowing things in or keeping them out. A gate implies control over one's territory. Like a door it can also be an opening into another person's domain, or into a whole new world of experience. In this way, 'gate' can also be a symbol for sexual invitation or barriers.

In the *Imago* location, the word suggests that my major conscious desires at the time were for new (sexual?) experience or for a greater sense of control over my own personal space. Both of these suggestions ring true. Although I engaged very little in any kind of direct sexual pursuit, I was always conscious of the possibility of new romantic involvements and I hoped that I would eventually find someone with whom I might share a life. I was, however, also aware that I was going through a particularly vulnerable phase emotionally and that I must guard against becoming involved 'on the rebound'. Partly because of this, I felt the need to exercise greater caution and control in allowing others (especially women) to get close.

In a more positive vein, 'gate' signifies the anticipated opening up of fresh opportunities. This included the possibility not only of new romantic attachments but also of furthering my academic and leisure activities, unhindered by the domestic pressures that inevitably exist when living with another person. Interestingly, shortly afterwards my academic research took on a new vitality that I had not experienced for several years. Although to some extent this may have been an attempt to compensate for emotional failure, the work carried out over the next few months was, in terms of my career, of considerable significance.

Shadow = 'devil'

Because *Shadow* indicates repressed or unrecognized aspects of our character or experience, this key always presents something of a difficulty when it comes to interpretation. Thus to the extent that our 'darker' side is not fully available to consciousness, we can never obtain a clear or direct view of what is going on under the surface. Instead we generally have to approach our *Shadow* indirectly, either by considering oblique or symbolic associations to the key word or by asking ourselves in what way it may reflect qualities that we strongly object to in others.

I do not have any strong theological belief in the existence of the devil. For me, 'devil' represents a symbolic caricature of all that is evil and despicable in humankind. As such it encompasses, for example, hatred, violence, anger, domination, ignorance, greed, vanity, laziness and exploitation. This key calls me to question the extent to which these 'demonic' characteristics may be tendencies in my own being that need to be recognized, accepted and worked upon, rather than denied or projected onto others.

At the time when I completed this matrix, perhaps the most necessary realization was exactly how much pain and anger I was repressing in relation to the break-up of my marriage. Rightly or wrongly I felt badly let down and, without being aware of it, a part of me was seething with rage at what in many ways I had allowed or forced to happen. Only by acknowledging these feelings could I begin genuinely to accept and learn from my situation, thereby freeing myself finally from the emotional chains that I still felt were binding me.

This key may also be warning me to look carefully at the motives behind my current activities, particularly in my relations with women. Thus perhaps I needed to recognize those 'devilish' aspects of my character that, if allowed to control the situation, could lead to corruption or mischief. With hindsight, I am aware of several occasions when my untimely sexual aspirations interfered with or perverted attempts to form relationships with women.

Spectre = 'self'

'Self' is derived from the combination of 'nevertheless – alone'. Its meaning seems, therefore, to refer primarily to feelings of loneliness and isolation. The key indicates that my major conscious anxieties at this time centred around the fact that I was now living alone in an area of the country where I had no family and few friends. Furthermore, I had to accept the possibility that this state of affairs might persist indefinitely. There were, of course, moments of despair and self-pity when I doubted that matters would ever improve. Yet there was also a basic optimism and sense of self-worth that carried me through these difficult times.

'Self' in the *Spectre* location also implies that my lack of success in personal relationships may be due to a tendency to 'keep myself to myself', to be overly self-reliant or self-contained, and perhaps to resist overtures of friendship from another. A major problem with my marriage, I now recognize, had been my insularity and inability or unwillingness to communicate openly with my wife about even trivial, everyday issues. I had also become much too wrapped up in my work and academic research while failing to express any kind of effective interest in my wife's career or recreations. Although, since my separation, I had made attempts to be more outgoing and to forge new friendships, I was still basically reserved, uncommunicative and self-absorbed.

Station = 'maze'

'Maze' is another particularly significant symbol. It indicates not only a state of confusion, difficulty or alienation, but also the possibility of resolution, discovery, escape or home-coming. In this respect, 'maze' provides a most interesting commentary upon my then situation and sense of identity. Clearly this was a time of major crisis in my life. Recent events had disrupted any personal equilibrium I might have felt and it seemed that I had entered a new and confusing world of unknown dimensions. In practice, therefore, one of my main problems was in deciding exactly what to do with myself, which alternatives to choose, what path to follow, whom to befriend.

Yet this was also a time of fresh and exciting opportunities and of singular challenge. I believed that I was starting out on an important adventure through which I would eventually 'find' myself and, hopefully, other people. The maze has been recognized as a powerful symbol for the approach to the unconscious and for the processes by which the individual 'hero' may come to a realization of the archetype of the self (see, for example, Jung, 1964). Thus by courageously and vigilantly weaving our way through a labyrinth of vast complexity and hidden dangers we may finally discover the true centre of our being, to reap the ultimate reward of genuine selfhood.

'Maze' in the *Station* location is therefore a highly optimistic sign. This key seems to be promising me that no matter how uncertain and formidable my present situation may appear, by persevering bravely and by maintaining personal vigilance, I shall finally win through, discover a great boon, and come out of this episode whole and strong.

Battle = 'transcend'

Whereas *Station* implies that my situation was one both of confusion and of great opportunity, *Battle* indicates the major moral task that needs to be performed in order to realize the goal of my quest. 'Transcend' suggests that the most difficult and important achievement will involve a going beyond or above present constraints.

Because this word is derived from 'flood – ego' I believe it mainly signifies the need to transcend egocentric concerns and to take a much more broad, noble or generous perspective. It is clear from much of the previous discussion that I was particularly self-preoccupied at this period of my life. This is understandable and almost inevitable for anyone experiencing a major life crisis such as separation, divorce, bereavement or unemployment. At these times we become blinkered by our own problems, see everything in terms of its effects on ourselves and are continually examining and re-evaluating our concept of self. This key therefore seems to be advising me to concentrate rather less on my own predicament or on purely personal needs and interests. Instead I should attempt to go out from the self by investing genuine concern in other people or in wider social, humanitarian or spiritual issues.

Destiny = 'rebirth'

'Rebirth' strikes me as a profound and wonderfully optimistic conclusion to this matrix. It expresses clearly the basic awareness I had at the time that any final resolution of my situation would involve a fundamental transformation in my approach to life. Thus the key indicates the need to throw off the shackles of the past and to make a completely fresh start, unhindered by the haunting memories of former ties. Perhaps most obviously this may have pointed to the necessity of making a clean, final emotional break with my wife.

Yet 'rebirth' indicates more than the need to break with the past. Crucially it suggests that I must undergo a total reassessment and overhaul of current attitudes, beliefs and personal tendencies. Something very basic in the structure of my personality will have to change before I can achieve any kind of completion, fulfilment or psychological well-being. Only through a personal metamorphosis, by being reborn or reformed, may new creative vitality be found.

STAGE 5: DIALECTICAL RELATIONSHIPS

The key interpretations outlined in Stage 4 present a fairly full and consistent picture of my psychological situation at the time. Each key has given up its secrets readily and it may appear that there is little more to be learned. A consideration of dialectical relationships in the matrix may, however, give additional clarification on certain points. In this respect, the following observations seem most relevant.

Guide vs *Shadow* = *Soul*

The tension or opposition here seems to be between (a) inner qualities of spirituality, responsiveness, emotional sensitivity and idealism (*Guide* = 'water') and (b) unrecognized tendencies towards materialism, coldness and emotional domination (*Shadow* = 'devil'). Basically it appears that my gaze may be so strongly drawn in the direction of goodness and light that I fail to see my own inner darkness or corruption. By ignoring or repressing these characteristics, I am unable to come to any satisfactory resolution of the conflict in my being between the forces of light and darkness or good and evil. As a result, my inner world remains confused, turbulent and out of control (*Soul* = 'whirlpool').

Imago vs *Spectre* = *Persona*

'Gate' (*Imago*) and 'self' (*Spectre*) imply a conflict between (a) the desire for new social and sexual experience (moderated, however, by the need to be cautious and discriminating) and (b) the fear of remaining alone and isolated. It seems that I want to open up to others, and to accept their offers of friendship or love, yet at the same time I feel it is important to be selective in my choice of friends. This in turn leads me to worry that by being too fussy or circumspect I may alienate myself completely from others, thus becoming condemned to a solitary and friendless existence. The resolution of this conflict is represented by 'truth' in the *Persona* location. This appears to confirm that my conscious obsession with perfection may be at the root of the problem I have in developing relationships. Perhaps I am overly critical and rejecting of others who do not reach the high standards I profess. To the extent that I am unwilling to accept people as they are, with all their faults and idiosyncrasies, then it will be impossible for me to find friendship or love and I will inevitably become isolated.

Guide vs *Imago* = *Giant*

This dialectical relationship expresses clearly the contradiction between my inner and outer yearnings. Inwardly I am drawn towards spiritual matters and romantic ideals (*Guide* = 'water') yet my conscious external goals seem to be for new experience (social or sexual) and for increased control over my personal life and relationships (*Imago* = 'gate').

The link I have formed (*Giant* = 'flood') suggests, I believe, a way forward that may help to integrate these conflicting needs. This involves opening up both to my own emotional experience and to the presence of others. Emotionally and socially, it seems, I have erected high walls of pretence behind which I am protected from threat yet which also imprison and frustrate me. Release can come only by tearing down these fortifications and becoming fully open to both inner and outer worlds.

Shadow vs *Spectre* = *Dwarf*

The tension or opposition between 'devil' (*Shadow*) and 'self' (*Spectre*) is not immediately apparent. On closer examination I believe that the major conflict implied here is between (a) repressed feelings of anger that are projected onto others and (b) a conscious tendency to self-pity or self-blame. It seems that whereas conscious anxieties focus on myself, unconsciously I harbour deep-seated anger or resentment towards others. 'Ego' in the *Dwarf* location provides an interesting resolution, suggesting that feelings of both anger and self-pity are founded upon a basically ego-centric perspective that exacerbates my problems and frustrates progress.

Another aspect of the opposition between *Spectre* and *Shadow* may be a tension that exists within me between (a) a fear of loneliness and isolation and (b) a tendency to corrupt or destroy relationships by allowing unrecognized faults or weaknesses in my character to sabotage events. It seems that, although I dread the thought of remaining alone, my own darker nature may drive me into this corner. Once again, *Dwarf* indicates that it is my 'ego' or self-centredness that lies at the root of this conflict.

Soul vs *Persona* = *Station*

'Whirlpool' (*Soul*) and 'truth' (*Persona*) point clearly to a contrast between inner turmoil and outer poise. Emotionally I was in a state of great confusion at the time. Yet outwardly, or on the surface, all seemed stable and under control. 'Maze' (*Station*) suggests that to resolve this contradiction between my inner and outer personalities, I need to recognize the challenge that my situation presented. In facing up to my own emotional confusion honestly, and in viewing my current difficulties as problems to be solved, I may finally discover a deeper truth about myself.

Giant vs Dwarf = Battle

The opposition here seems to be between (a) the expansiveness and new vitality of 'flood' (*Giant*) and (b) the restriction and deadness of 'ego' (*Dwarf*). These two sets of forces provide the dynamic framework upon which hang the possibilities of progress or stagnation. The moral crux is represented by 'transcend' (*Battle*), suggesting that my major personal task is to go beyond egocentric concerns and to overcome the sense of separateness that is alienating me from others.

Station vs Battle = Destiny

The contrast between 'maze' (*Station*) and 'transcend' (*Battle*) is that between (a) being enclosed within the limited territory of my own 'self' and its current problems and (b) the need to go beyond or above present restrictions and preoccupations. 'Rebirth' (*Destiny*) suggests that in order to come to a final resolution of this conflict (which reiterates and expands upon that between *Giant* and *Dwarf*) I will need to undergo some kind of major personal transformation or spiritual initiation. A clean break with both the past and present is indicated, a laying of personal ghosts and a relinquishing of the crutches that support my tottering sense of identity. Above all I must be willing to start over, to be 'born again' into a new life of changed priorities and fresh opportunities.

STAGE 6: DEVELOPMENTAL RELATIONSHIPS

Outer development (*Spectre – Persona – Imago*)

Outer development is indicated by the sequence 'self – truth – gate'. This suggests that in order for progress to be made in my public or social life, I first need to confront directly the conflict between my fear of loneliness and my tendency towards insularity and solitary pursuits (*Spectre* = 'self'). I must realize that my self-absorption and failure to communicate with others are necessarily preventing me from forming meaningful relationships.

'Truth' in the *Persona* location seems to represent a double-edged sword. Thus in one respect my cold intellectualism, conscious obsession with perfection and hypercritical rejection of others all serve to distance me from society and to frustrate attempts at closeness. Yet paradoxically one of my main virtues seems to be an apparent honesty, genuineness and openness that other people often respond to positively and that may encourage them to talk to me freely and intimately. 'Truth' seems to be telling me that I need to face up to this contradiction in my outer personality.

Specifically, I need to work to develop the positive attributes that 'truth' may contribute to my character, while moderating negative tendencies. In this way I may eventually succeed in achieving the conscious goals that are symbolized by 'gate' (*Imago*), such as new social and sexual experience, true discrimination in relationships and a sense of control over my personal life.

Inner development (*Shadow – Soul – Guide*)

Even though this matrix was completed when I was 34 years of age, almost exactly at Jung's supposed 'midlife crisis' separating the stages of outer and inner development, many of the difficulties that are indicated relate to problems of re-adapting to the world of relationships. In this respect outer development would seem to be the major conscious priority at the time. On the other hand, these problems with relationships may well be the result of a failure to come to terms with certain neglected or repressed inner tendencies that had perhaps begun to assert themselves at this critical period. For this reason, as well as in the interests of completeness, it is important to examine the process of inner development.

Inner development is represented by the sequence 'devil – whirlpool – water'. The first stage in the process of individuation is therefore for me to focus upon and recognize my own repressed corrupt, wicked or devilish tendencies such as arrogance, anger, exploitativeness or lust (*Shadow* = 'devil').

Following on from this, I may begin to confront the anima projections (*Soul* = 'whirlpool') that in many ways seem to be at the root of the difficulties I have experienced in my relations with women. In particular, I need to question deeply the sense in which I may see the women to whom I am attracted as magnetic and fascinating but also as potentially dangerous sirens who might yet lure me to my doom. Adopting a Jungian perspective, it is by facing up to these largely unconscious attitudes towards women that I may discover something important about the nature of my own inner femininity.

These anima projections clearly represent an area in which major personal work is suggested. Eventually, however, it may become possible for me to confront aspects of my mana personality (*Guide* = 'water'). This key indicates that the third stage of individuation will involve the full recognition of my inner yearnings towards romantic ideals, spirituality and emotional responsiveness. In particular, it will be important for me to learn to accept these tendencies as major inner drives that provide strength and direction in my life, while at the same time avoiding the temptation to allow them to dominate me completely. Instead I will need to incorporate this aspect of my nature coherently into the total fabric of the self.

Development of Self (*Station – Battle – Destiny*)

To a large extent, development of the self is contingent upon making adequate progress in the areas of outer and inner development. Self-development cannot, therefore, meaningfully be considered in isolation. Yet by studying the progression from *Station*, through *Battle*, to *Destiny*, some useful general pointers may be established.

Development of self is represented by the sequence 'maze – transcend – rebirth'. 'Maze' indicates that the starting point of my quest for selfhood is a position of uncertainty, choice and personal crisis, but also of opportunity. As such, it is important for me to recognize the unique possibilities for personal development inherent in the situation I was faced with. Although times were difficult, an optimistic and positive attitude is called for.

Having adopted this forward-looking perspective, the next and crucial stage will entail an intense struggle to transcend personal constraints and egocentric concerns. In this way I may become able not only to view my inner world with greater openness and objectivity, but also to make a more genuine attempt to establish meaningful relationships with others. Finally, 'rebirth' offers the promise that as a result of this personal struggle I may ultimately undergo some kind of profound and revitalizing transformation.

STAGE 7: SYNTHESIZING THE MATRIX

The analysis presented in the previous sections gives a detailed and coherent picture of my situation in 1984. Because of this, and in order not to overtax or bore the reader, only a very brief summary is necessary.

The major themes of the matrix point to a fundamental conflict in my being between (a) personal limitation, isolation, and a concern with protecting my ego, and (b) the need to open up both to inner emotional experience and to other people, to relax and to transcend egocentric attitudes and preoccupations.

Particular problems that the matrix indicates I should address focus upon the following:

1 An inferior extraverted attitude that results in immature expressions of sociability.
2 A failure to differentiate adequately the feeling function, resulting in difficulties in understanding my own emotional experience.
3 Repressed sensation that may cause personal neglect, obsessional interests, compulsive habits and an inability to relax or to enjoy the simple pleasures of life.
4 Repressed feelings of pain, anger and anxiety relating especially to the break-up of my marriage.
5 A dread of loneliness and isolation.

6 Confusion and difficulty in my relationships with women that may hinge critically upon certain anima projections.
7 Arrogance, a perfectionistic streak, the sense of intellectual superiority, insularity and excessive self-reliance – all of which may lead me to reject overtures of friendship from others.
8 A tendency to allow selfish interests, sexual desires or the need for control to corrupt or destroy attempts at developing relationships.

At the same time, there are several positive aspects to the matrix that ought to be encouraged and developed. These include indications of emotional sensitivity, idealism, personal integrity and powerful spiritual interests. Most importantly, however, the matrix points clearly and optimistically to the potential achievement of some kind of profound psychological breakthrough, emotional catharsis or personal transformation involving a new beginning and fresh opportunities.

POSTSCRIPT

Even as I write this chapter, several years since completing the matrix upon which it is based, I am struck with the sometimes frightening accuracy of the personal analysis it provides. Although several of the issues to which the matrix relates have become rather less urgent in the intervening period, have been resolved to some degree or have been overtaken by events (for example, I have remarried and now have a child) many characteristics and problems remain to haunt me. Personal growth, it seems, is neither easy nor quick.

8 Analysing change

REPEATING THE WATCHWORD TECHNIQUE

Watchword often impresses people most on their first attempt, when they have completed the matrix with no prior knowledge of its underlying structure. Once we become aware of Watchword's system there is always the possibility that later exercises will be influenced, consciously or unconsciously, by the expectations we have acquired. This is, of course, why it is important that you should not reveal Watchword's exact purpose or structural principles to your friends.

Although bias is always possible with subsequent exercises, experience has shown that the technique can be repeated to provide meaningful analyses of change in our patterns of experience. Significantly, provided that no deliberate attempt is made to influence the outcome, later matrices are often strikingly similar to earlier ones. This consistency is usually reflected most clearly in the basic psychological type exhibited in the matrix and also in the dominant theme. It is also not uncommon to find close parallels between the words that are written on separate occasions in specific key locations. In contrast, the original sixteen root words are generally very different in each case. These stabilities in the matrix provide powerful evidence, I believe, that the Watchword technique taps something important and fundamental in the person's psychological make-up.

As an example of this consistency, consider Matrices 42, 43 and 44. These were all completed by the same person (Susan) on three separate occasions. There was a seven-month gap between Matrices 42 and 43, and eleven months between Matrices 43 and 44. Again, to aid interpretation of these matrices, the eight words outside the main rectangle are also shown.

In terms of psychological type, the three matrices are all variations upon extraverted intuitive feeling (although there are also traces of introversion). Matrix 42 may be characterized as EN(F), Matrix 43 as EF(N) or ENF and Matrix 44 as EN(F).

The overall theme of each matrix is also basically constant, reflecting a conflict between (a) romantic idealism and the desire for friendship, happiness, order and personal fulfilment and (b) feelings of alienation,

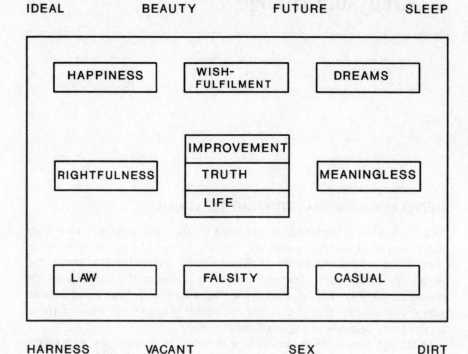

IDEAL BEAUTY FUTURE SLEEP

HAPPINESS	WISH-FULFILMENT	DREAMS
RIGHTFULNESS	IMPROVEMENT TRUTH LIFE	MEANINGLESS
LAW	FALSITY	CASUAL

HARNESS VACANT SEX DIRT

Matrix 42 (Susan, no. 1)

meaninglessness, chaos and loneliness that may, in turn, be linked to social or sexual anxiety.

Although there are significant changes in several of the key words, other keys show relatively stable or consonant meanings on at least two occasions. Notable among these are *Giant* ('wish-fulfilment – wish') and *Imago* ('dreams – romance').

People sometimes ask how often they should repeat the Watchword technique. Because the system is basically a method for analysing one's current psychological situation, the simple answer to this question is: whenever you desire a fresh psychological analysis and have reason to suspect that important changes have occurred since your last matrix. The frequency with which exercises are meaningful will clearly differ from one person to the next. It will also depend upon the extent to which your personal circumstances are static or changing. As a rough guide, however, it is rarely productive to repeat Watchword at intervals of less than one or two months. On the other hand if you are simply experimenting with the technique, or if you have difficulty interpreting a particular matrix, then more frequent exercises may be indicated.

SHINE   GOOD   LIFE   SOFT

```
┌──────────────────────────────────────────────────────┐
│                                                        │
│   ┌──────────┐      ┌──────────┐      ┌──────────┐    │
│   │   CARE   │      │  AMITY   │      │  PEACE   │    │
│   └──────────┘      └──────────┘      └──────────┘    │
│                                                        │
│                     ┌──────────────┐                  │
│                     │ FRIENDSHIP   │                  │
│   ┌──────────┐      ├──────────────┤    ┌──────────┐  │
│   │AFFECTION │      │  DISTANCE    │    │ CONCERN  │  │
│   └──────────┘      ├──────────────┤    └──────────┘  │
│                     │   WARY       │                  │
│                     └──────────────┘                  │
│                                                        │
│   ┌──────────┐      ┌──────────┐      ┌──────────┐    │
│   │  TOUCH   │      │ FRIGIDITY│      │ ANXIOUS  │    │
│   └──────────┘      └──────────┘      └──────────┘    │
│                                                        │
└──────────────────────────────────────────────────────┘
```

HANDS   TENDER   COLD   HAPPY

Matrix 43 (Susan, no. 2)

Although Watchword should not be repeated too often it is necessary, in order to trace the course of personal development, to complete a new matrix at approximately regular intervals – say, every six months or every year. If the exercise is carried out less frequently, it becomes difficult to identify the patterns of stability or processes of change. It will be unclear, for example, whether two widely spaced and very different matrices reflect genuine development or mere inconsistency.

COMPARING MATRICES

When Watchword is repeated, the latest matrix will of course provide an analysis of your current situation. Any new matrix may therefore be interpreted fully using the procedures already described. More than this, however, it is also possible to examine patterns of change and stability. To do this, the later matrix should be considered in conjunction with the earlier matrix.

BLIND   EXTRAVAGANCE   PEACE   SUPPER

DESIRE	WISH	ROMANCE
NEED	UNFULFILMENT / ALONE / COMPANY	LONELY
DEVELOPMENT	REGRESSION	DISAPPEAR

PROCESS   SEQUENCE   FAMILY   FLOOD

Matrix 44 (Susan, no. 3)

Psychological type

To begin, you should compare the psychological type indicated for each matrix (see Chapter 5). Although it is to be expected that an individual's type will remain fairly constant, when change is apparent this can often be personally significant. Such change normally indicates either (a) that the person is learning consciously to differentiate and express the dominant attitude or function type, (b) that the person is becoming aware of and learning to express one or both auxiliary functions, or the other attitude type, or (c) that, in response to the demands of current circumstances, there has been a temporary change in the relative emphasis given to the dominant and auxiliary functions.

In the case of Susan, the major change in typing occurs in Matrix 43. Whereas Matrices 42 and 44 both indicate extraverted intuitive feeling, with intuition as the dominant function, Matrix 43 reveals a much more salient feeling function. This suggests that Susan's basic type remains EN(F), but that when completing Matrix 43 she may have been going through a phase in which feeling was powerfully stimulated. Interestingly, it was at this very time that Susan started up what was to become a significant new romantic involvement.

One important general conclusion that can be drawn from Susan's example is that you should be wary of making final judgements about psychological type on the basis of completing only one or two matrices. Several successive Watchword exercises may be required before it is possible to determine clearly a person's basic type or to decide whether apparent changes represent temporary aberrations or a more lasting and fundamental psychological achievement.

Dominant theme

After psychological type, the next matter to consider is change or stability in the dominant theme of the matrix. In practice this will reveal whether or not there has been any significant movement in the person's conscious preoccupations.

With Susan, Matrix 42 indicates that her earlier concerns centred around a perceived need to achieve happiness, truth and self-improvement against a background of conflict between (a) romantic fantasies or idealistic dreams and (b) a sense of meaninglessness and falsehood. Matrix 43 focuses much more clearly upon the interpersonal domain. Thus Susan now seems to be absorbed in problems of achieving romantic friendship. Matrix 44, completed nearly a year later, is in many ways a compromise between the two earlier matrices. Susan seems to have returned to the question of how to achieve personal development and fulfilment, but this question is now framed more specifically in terms of the conflict between isolation and intimacy.

Key interpretation

Having examined changes in dominant theme, you should next compare the words that have been written on different occasions at each key location. In this way it will be possible to see whether a key has retained aspects of the original meaning or whether significant change has occurred. Keys showing a clear change are especially important because they generally indicate either (a) psychological forces or tendencies that the individual is confused about or (b) those aspects of the person's character or situation that are, or have been, undergoing major development.

In Susan's matrices, most of the keys exhibit both a general consistency in flavour and a seemingly interpretable and interesting development of meaning. To consider just one example, the sequence of words at *Persona* ('meaningless – concern – lonely') suggests, firstly, that Susan views her outer personality as being a continuing source of worry and difficulty. The first matrix ('meaningless') indicates that Susan feels alienated from her public self or from the social roles that she may be required to adopt. In the second matrix ('concern') this general sense of alienation and falseness seems to have become more fully acknowledged *emotionally*. This is an important achievement because it means that Susan is beginning consciously to accept the feelings of anxiety and unhappiness that she has about her outer life. In the third matrix ('lonely') the source of these anxieties is clearly identified as the problem of maintaining intimate relationships. Through recognizing in specific and concrete terms the nature and basis of her worries, Susan may hopefully become able to tackle these difficulties head-on.

When a key is highly inconsistent, it will be necessary to interpret each occasion separately. In this way, although it may be impossible to establish a lasting theme or clear developmental progression, you should be able to identify various aspects of the key that are of at least temporary significance. In Susan's case, the key which appears to show the greatest variability of meaning is *Shadow* ('law – touch – development'), indicating an inability to differentiate clearly the darker side of her character. The words at this location might suggest, however, that Susan's shadow includes a feeling of being restricted ('law'), a fear of physical intimacy ('touch'), and worries about a lack of progress ('development').

Dialectical and developmental relationships

When comparing successive matrices, interpretation may be clarified and elaborated by examining changes in both dialectical and developmental relationships. In particular, changes in the three developmental relationships (i.e., outer development, inner development and development of self) should be studied carefully. This is because these changes may help to determine (a) the areas in which developmental requirements have yet to be clearly identified and (b) the areas in which important personal growth is taking place.

With Susan, the requirements of outer development (*Spectre – Persona – Imago*) appear to be basically constant across matrices. These keys indicate the need to face up to conscious anxieties, especially those concerning intimate relationships (*Spectre*), to overcome the sense of alienation and isolation that characterizes the public self (*Persona*) and finally to actualize romantic dreams (*Imago*). Significantly, the three matrices also suggest that outer development is becoming increasingly defined in concrete terms. Thus, in comparison with the first two matrices, both of which are relatively abstract in this respect, the third matrix focuses much more specifically upon the problems of achieving or maintaining a romantic involvement with another person.

In contrast, inner development (*Shadow – Soul – Guide*) seems to be an area in which Susan is somewhat confused. This is suggested not only by the lack of consistency in *Shadow* already considered, but also by the variation in *Soul* ('rightfulness – affection – need'). It appears, therefore, that Susan may be unclear about the nature of her basic inner personality, emotional situation or animus. In turn this may result in difficulties in her relationships with men. She may, for example, project onto them her own inconsistencies or needs.

The development of self (*Station – Battle – Destiny*) also varies in Susan's matrices. In general, however, each matrix emphasizes the need for personal development or self-improvement. In Matrix 42 this is expressed in fairly abstract terms, whereas Matrices 43 and 44 are clearly orientated towards the problems of achieving fulfilment in relationships. This reinforces the point made earlier about the apparent progressive concretizing of aspects of Susan's experience.

COMPOSITE MATRICES

In addition to comparing a later with an earlier matrix, it is possible to derive from these a composite matrix that describes the deeper, more constant features of one's personality. To do this, take a blank matrix form and proceed according to the following steps. As an example, Matrix 45 is the composite matrix completed by Susan from Matrices 42 and 43.

Step 1

Identify the two words (phrases) that appear in the *Guide* location of the earlier and later matrices and write them in the two boxes *directly above* this location on the new form. Repeat this step for *Imago*.

Step 2

Identify the two words (phrases) that appear in the *Shadow* location of the earlier and later matrices and write them in the two boxes *directly below* this location on the new form. Repeat this step for *Spectre*.

Step 3

Ignoring the earlier and later matrices, complete the composite matrix in the standard way, by working directly from the eight words or phrases written outside the main rectangle (see Chapter 2).

Interpreting composite matrices

Composite matrices indicate persisting qualities or tendencies in one's character or situation. As such they are especially useful for probing more deeply into the psyche and for identifying long-term processes or fundamental sources of strength or difficulty. Essentially they tap more directly than standard matrices the 'deep structure' of personality. Because of this they are generally less helpful in providing specific insight into one's

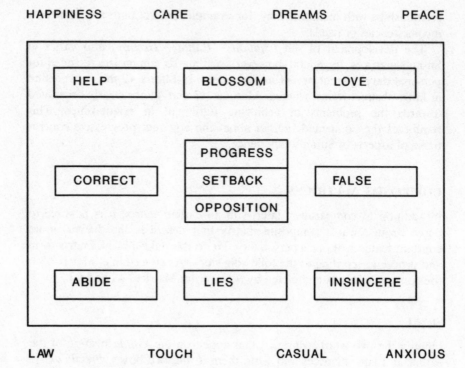

Matrix 45 (Susan, composite 1)

current affairs. They are, however, excellent at stripping the psyche down to reveal its essential qualities.

Composite matrices may be interpreted in the usual fashion, taking into account psychological type, dominant theme, the significance of individual keys and both dialectical and developmental relationships. Interpretation should always recognize, however, that a composite matrix is one step removed from the person's immediate situation or experience. For this reason, composites should not normally be interpreted in isolation but should be used to supplement conclusions drawn from the component matrices.

Even without a detailed examination of Susan's composite, it is evident that important aspects of her basic character have been clearly identified. In particular, the matrix reinforces the fundamental conflict between her desire for truth, love, personal development and fulfilment on the one hand and her recognition of opposition, failure and inadequacy on the other.

CARE	DESIRE	PEACE	ROMANCE

```
┌─────────────────────────────────────────────────────────────┐
│  ┌──────────────┐   ┌──────────────┐   ┌──────────────┐      │
│  │   WANT       │   │   WISH       │   │   LOVE       │      │
│  └──────────────┘   └──────────────┘   └──────────────┘      │
│                                                               │
│                     ┌──────────────┐                         │
│                     │   NEVER      │                         │
│  ┌──────────────┐   ├──────────────┤   ┌──────────────┐      │
│  │ FRIENDSHIP   │   │   LONELY     │   │   SINGLE     │      │
│  └──────────────┘   ├──────────────┤   └──────────────┘      │
│                     │   FRIEND     │                         │
│                     └──────────────┘                         │
│                                                               │
│  ┌──────────────┐   ┌──────────────┐   ┌──────────────┐      │
│  │  FAMILIAR    │   │ REPETITION   │   │   ALONE      │      │
│  └──────────────┘   └──────────────┘   └──────────────┘      │
└─────────────────────────────────────────────────────────────┘
```

TOUCH	DEVELOPMENT	ANXIOUS	DISAPPEAR

Matrix 46 (Susan, composite 2)

Composite series

When several standard matrices are completed over a period of time, it is also possible to derive a series of composite matrices that trace the deeper patterns of stability and change in personality or circumstances. Thus, whenever a new matrix is added, a further composite can be formed by connecting this latest matrix with the previous one. This procedure is shown in Susan's second composite (Matrix 46).

Whenever a new composite is formed, it should first be interpreted in conjunction with the two standard matrices from which it is derived. Having done this it may then be compared with any earlier composites. Generally it is expected that successive composite matrices will be more similar to each other than are standard matrices. For this reason, particular attention should be paid to any major changes that are indicated in composites.

Susan's second composite is significant because, unlike her earlier composite, it focuses in a much more concrete manner upon the conflict she is experiencing between isolation and intimacy (loneliness and friendship). Also the psychological typing of the second composite indicates a much stronger feeling function than is exhibited in her other matrices. Taken together, these facts suggest that Susan is going through an important phase of development in which she needs to come to terms with the problems associated with intimate relationships. Furthermore, it is through this experience that she may be learning to acknowledge and express her auxiliary feeling function.

Higher-order composites

If desired, pairs of composite matrices can themselves be combined to derive yet deeper 'second-order' composites. In theory it is possible to continue this process indefinitely, producing, for example, third-order composites from two second-order matrices. In practice, however, higher-order composites will usually add little of interest. For one thing they can be quite difficult to form, with people complaining that they run out of words to use. Also, higher-order composites tend to become repetitive, often reproducing more or less exactly the patterns of meaning revealed by lower-order composites.

9 Final thoughts

DOES WATCHWORD REALLY WORK?

Since developing the Watchword system, and while writing this book, I have been continually surprised and encouraged by the results that may be achieved with this simple technique. By using the method regularly and conscientiously it is possible, I believe, to gain a fascinating and valuable insight into the self and personal development.

Even though there is a basic inner logic to Watchword's structure, exactly how the method works in practice remains largely a mystery. I can certainly sympathize with people who might dismiss the technique as an absurdity. For, considered in purely rational terms, it may indeed seem unlikely that a penetrating psychological analysis can be derived using a procedure that starts with such apparently insignificant and unpromising material as the first words that come into one's head.

Yet this is perhaps not as implausible as it might appear. The use of some form of word association is a technique with a long and honoured history within psychoanalytic circles. Furthermore, even rationally, it will be conceded that personal characteristics must somehow influence the spontaneous generation of ideas. Essentially all that Watchword has done is to suggest certain ways in which this influence may operate. Thus words and associations that a person 'freely' produces are believed to be subtly modified by the individual's psychological type and by the archetypal (perhaps physiologically determined) significance of spatial location. Surely neither of these assumptions is particularly outrageous.

It is impossible to prove scientifically the accuracy of Watchword's self-analysis. Ultimately each person who uses the technique must decide whether or not it works in his or her individual case. There are, however, a few significant pointers which to my mind indicate the basic validity of the method.

Most important is the general stability of the Watchword matrix over time. Matrices that have been completed months or even years apart are usually very similar in terms of both psychological type and dominant theme. Also it is quite common to find that words written on different occasions in particular key locations are remarkably consistent in meaning. Secondly, matrices are generally *recognizable*. By this I mean that the matrix 'fits' the individual who has completed it. This fit is not simply the kind obtained with newspaper horoscopes, which are sweepingly vague and indiscriminating. In contrast, Watchword matrices are specific and personal. For example, if you were handed several matrices, each of which had been completed secretly by a different friend or member of your family, you would probably find it quite a simple task to identify who was responsible for each.

APPLICATIONS

Self-analysis

Watchword's primary purpose is to enable each individual to understand the psychological forces and tendencies operating at particular times within her or his own being. Such understanding is not merely an end in itself but rather is a means to the more important goal of self-realization. Thus by learning something about how we 'tick' we may hopefully become able to make more sensible and forward-looking life decisions.

I have emphasized throughout this book that Watchword is essentially a system of *self*-analysis in which it is important to derive your own interpretations. This does not mean, however, that you should not discuss your matrices with others. As long as you trust your friends to respect your disclosures and not to abuse or exploit the situation for their own ends, then it can be both interesting and helpful to exchange ideas about the possible significance of a matrix. You will certainly find that a fresh perspective often helps to trigger insights that perhaps you may not have achieved unaided.

Diagnosis and testing

On the question of whether it is possible to interpret another person's matrix, the answer must be a guarded 'yes'. In this book I have myself offered tentative interpretations for several matrices that were completed by other people. Although these analyses were made purely for the purpose of explaining general interpretive procedures rather than necessarily to provide an accurate psychological diagnosis of the other person, it is interesting that the picture that emerges of each individual is both coherent and believable. Also the very fact that people can be recognized from their matrices points to the ability of others to read from them something that is reliably true.

The easiest characteristics to identify in another person's matrix are psychological type and dominant theme. Provided we restrict ourselves to these features then, if desired, Watchword can be used as a vaguely objective 'test' of personality. Any other interpretations, especially concerning the significance of particular keys or the interrelationships within the matrix, must always be considered purely speculative unless confirmed by the testee.

Although Watchword may be used to make a partial diagnosis of another person, it was never my intention in writing this book that the method should become just another psychological test, to be used for categorizing or labelling other people, or for selecting them for particular tasks. I would be sorry indeed if this is how it ends up. The best insurance against this misuse of the technique is, I believe, to make the method widely known and freely available to the general public, rather than restricting its application to the psychological profession or other groups with vested interests. This is one reason why the book is not orientated specifically towards an academic or professional readership.

Once people become aware of the purpose and nature of the Watchword system they will, I trust, be cautious in allowing others to test them without good reason. Watchword is, after all, an intimate and psychologically deep procedure. We should therefore be circumspect and selective in our self-exposures. For the same reasons, I would be disturbed to hear that anyone was setting themselves up in the role of Watchword guru or expert interpreter of matrices, whether these services were being offered free of charge or on a commercial basis.

Counselling and therapy

One valid and potentially important application of Watchword is in the process of counselling or psychotherapy. By discussing your matrix with a counsellor or therapist who is familiar with and sympathetic towards the technique, you may find that important advances in self-understanding are achievable. It is my hope also that counsellors and therapists who read this book might themselves consider trying out the technique with their clients. Although the method is Jungian in its structure and emphasis, it reflects themes that are relevant in all therapeutic schools and systems. It may therefore be found of use and interest within a wide range of approaches.

Analysing relationships

A final use of the Watchword technique is in the analysis of interpersonal relationships. Knowing ourselves is clearly an important step towards making sense of our relations with others. In this way it is to be hoped that Watchword may facilitate greater understanding between friends, or partners, or members of a family. As well as discussing openly each person's matrices, in a general attempt to foster mutual awareness, there are a few specific matters that may also be considered. One of these is the relationship between psychological types.

Jung believed that much interpersonal conflict arises when a person of one type projects negative aspects of the inferior (unconscious) attitude or function onto people of this latter type. For example, as we have seen, extraverts may criticize introverts for being morose and unsociable, whereas introverts may grumble that extraverts are irresponsible and fickle. Similarly, a strongly intuitive person may have difficulty relating to a sensation type who may be seen as crude, materialistic or carnal, while a thinking person often has problems with feeling types, who perhaps seem overly sentimental. By discovering one's own psychological type and also that of the other person, each may become aware of, and therefore make allowances for, these unhelpful projections (see also Chapter 5).

With relationships between the sexes, an additional factor to consider is the role of anima or animus projections. Thus a male may project his own inner image of femininity (his anima) onto females. In the same way, a female may project her own unconscious masculinity (her animus) onto males. These projections cause two main problems. Firstly, we fail to recognize and express important characteristics within our own psyches. For example, a man may feel unable to act with sensitivity and gentleness, or to express emotional pain by weeping, while a woman may find it impossible to act assertively or to think rationally. Secondly, we see the other person not as he or she really is, but instead as a representation of our own idealized image of the supposed typical man or woman, or as a means of satisfying our own unconscious need for psychological completion. As a result we do not respond to members of the opposite sex as the rounded and complex individuals that they are, but rather as sexual stereotypes or two-dimensional caricatures of their gender.

In the Watchword matrix, these contrasexual tendencies are represented by *Soul*. By studying carefully the significance of this key, it may be possible to identify the nature of our anima or animus projections, to become aware of how they may adversely affect our relationships with the opposite sex, and thus to work on this aspect of our nature in a constructive fashion. If a matrix is completed by each member of a couple, they may also find it interesting and challenging to discuss their relationship in the light of possible interpretations of the words each has written in the *Soul* location. Be warned, however, that, while potentially this may be very rewarding, it can also be highly threatening to the relationship.

Interpersonal relationships are so complex and multifaceted that it is not possible to draw up hard and fast rules about compatibility between people. Although, generally speaking, it may be expected that opposite types, those with very different overall themes to their matrices or couples with conflicted anima-animus projections may find their relationships strained and difficult, it should also be remembered that personal growth can thrive on conflict and opposition. Indeed some people may be too compatible, with the result that their relationship becomes stale, unstimulating and frozen.

WATCHWORD'S MESSAGE

The most important message that the Watchword technique delivers is the need to understand the complexity of the self and of the factors that affect the individual's relationships with others. This understanding is never complete and, no matter how much self-awareness is achieved, personal and interpersonal difficulties will always remain. All that understanding the self implies is that we become better able to learn from and grow with our problems. We should therefore not expect that our lives can ever become completely peaceful and free from obstruction or complication. As one problem is resolved, another will surely arise. There is no final end, no ultimate resting place. All life is movement. The Watchword technique is but a single step towards an unreachable horizon.

Appendix
Blank matrix forms

These forms are for you to use. Full instructions for filling them in are given in Chapter 2. Please note that you should complete one matrix *before* studying the explanations of the Watchword technique provided in later chapters.

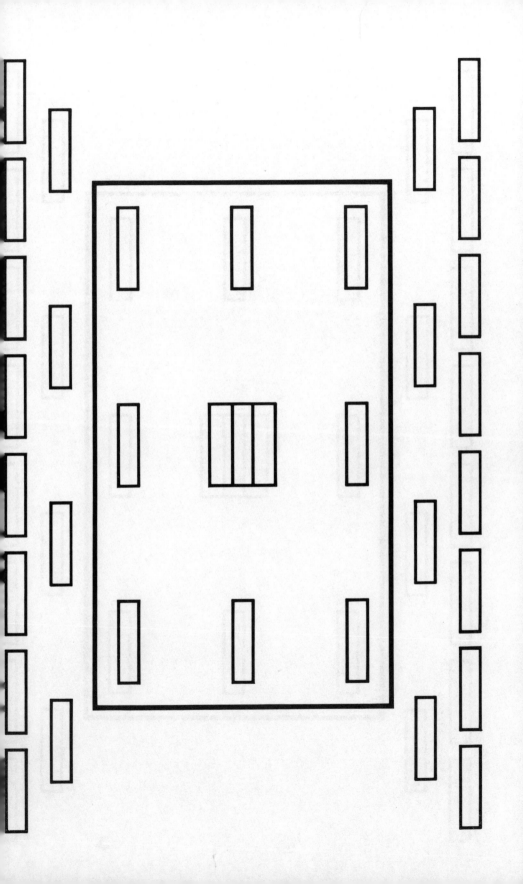

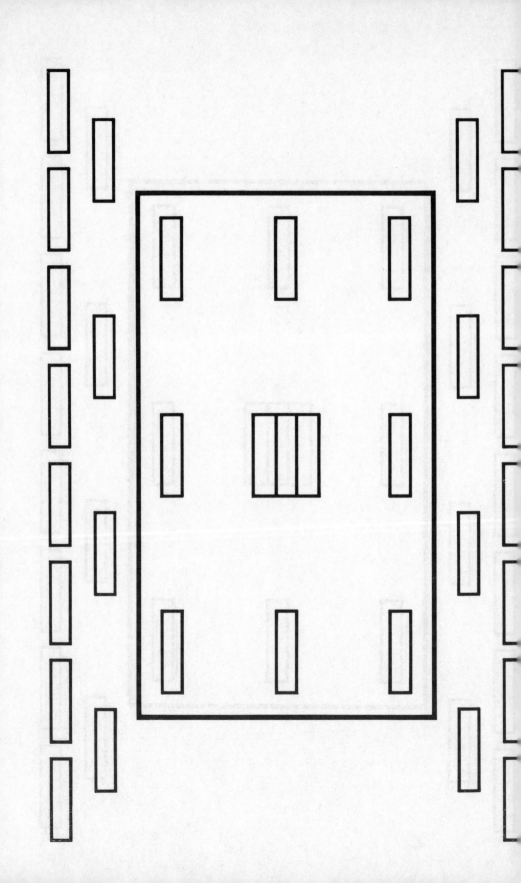

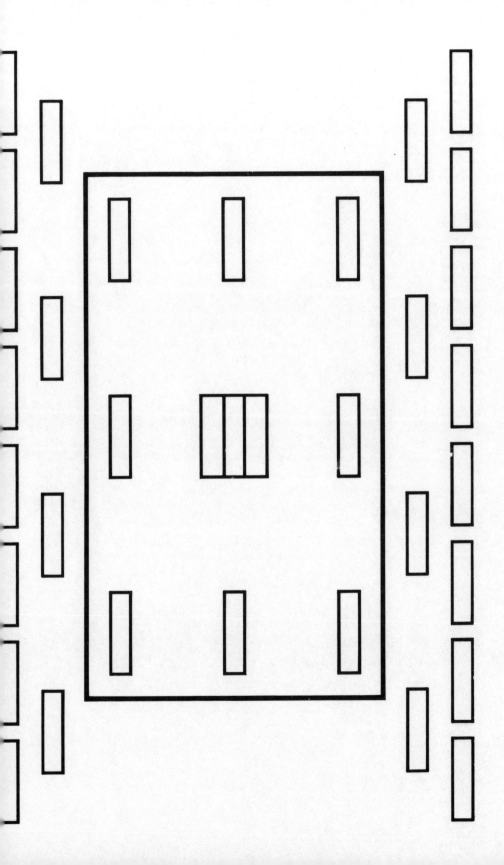

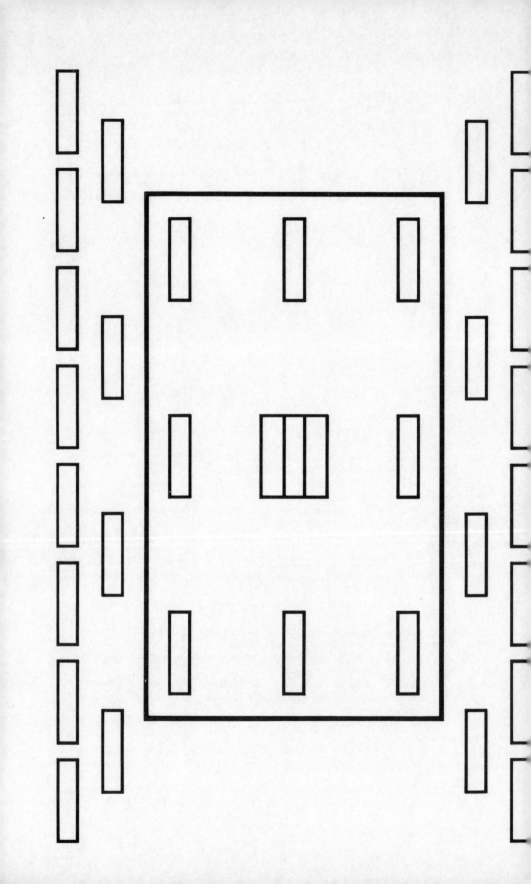

Bibliography

Anastasi, A. (1982) *Psychological Testing*, 5th edn, New York: Macmillan.
Annett, M. (1985) *Left, Right, Hand and Brain*, London: Lawrence Erlbaum.
Barsley, M. (1966) *The Left-Handed Book*, London: Souvenir Press.
—— (1970) *Left-Handed Man in a Right-Handed World*, London: Pitman.
Bradshaw, J.L. and Nettleton, N.C. (1981) 'The nature of hemispheric special-
ization in man', *The Behavioral and Brain Sciences* 4: 51–91.
Campbell, J. (1975) *The Hero with a Thousand Faces*, London: Sphere Books.
—— (1976a) *The Masks of God: Primitive Mythology*, Harmondsworth,
Middlesex: Penguin Books.
—— (1976b) *The Masks of God: Creative Mythology*, Harmondsworth,
Middlesex: Penguin Books.
Cirlot, J.E. (1971) *A Dictionary of Symbols*, 2nd edn, London: Routledge &
Kegan Paul.
Corballis, M.C. and Beale, I.L. (1983) *The Ambivalent Mind: The Neuro-
psychology of Left and Right*, Chicago: Nelson-Hall.
Daniels, M. (1982) 'The development of the concept of self-actualization in the
writings of Abraham Maslow', *Current Psychological Reviews* 2, 1: 61–76.
—— (1984) 'The relationship between moral development and self-actualization',
Journal of Moral Education 13, 1: 25–30.
—— (1988) 'The myth of self-actualization', *Journal of Humanistic Psychology*
28, 1: 7–38.
Dawson, E.R. (1909) *The Causation of Sex*, London: H.K. Lewis.
Freud, S. (1971) *The Complete Introductory Lectures on Psychoanalysis*, London:
George Allen & Unwin.
Gesell, A. and Ames, L.B. (1947) 'The development of handedness', *Journal of
Genetic Psychology* 70: 155–175.
Gimbutas, M. (1989) *The Language of the Goddess*, London: Thames & Hudson.
Gooch, S. (1975) *Total Man*, London: Sphere Books.
Greene, L. (1986) *Relating: An Astrological Guide to Living with Others*, Welling-
borough, Northamptonshire: Aquarian Press.
Gurdjieff, G.I. (1974) *All and Everything, 1st Series: An Objectively Impartial
Criticism of the Life of Man, or Beelzebub's Tales to His Grandson*, London:
Routledge & Kegan Paul.
Jacobi, J. (1968) *The Psychology of C.G. Jung*, 7th edn, London: Routledge &
Kegan Paul.
Jongbloet, P.H. (1983) 'Menses and moon phases, ovulation and seasons, vitality
and month of birth', *Developmental Medicine and Child Neurology* 25, 4: 527–
531.
Jung, C.G. (1954) *The Development of Personality*, London: Routledge & Kegan
Paul. (Collected Works of C.G. Jung, Vol. 17).

—— (ed.) (1964) *Man and His Symbols*, New York: Dell.

—— (1966) *Two Essays on Analytical Psychology*, 2nd edn, London: Routledge & Kegan Paul. (Collected Works of C.G. Jung, Vol. 7).

—— (1968a) *The Archetypes and the Collective Unconscious*, 2nd edn, London: Routledge & Kegan Paul. (Collected Works of C.G. Jung, Vol. 9, Part I).

—— (1968b) *Aion: Researches in the Phenomenology of the Self*, 2nd edn, London: Routledge & Kegan Paul. (Collected Works of C.G. Jung, Vol. 9, Part II).

—— (1968c) *Psychology and Alchemy*, 2nd edn, London: Routledge & Kegan Paul. (Collected Works of C.G. Jung, Vol. 12).

—— (1968d) *Alchemical Studies*, London: Routledge & Kegan Paul. (Collected Works of C.G. Jung, Vol. 13).

—— (1969) *The Structure and Dynamics of the Psyche*, 2nd edn, London: Routledge & Kegan Paul. (Collected Works of C.G. Jung, Vol. 8).

—— (1971) *Psychological Types*, London: Routledge & Kegan Paul. (Collected Works of C.G. Jung, Vol. 6).

—— (1976) *The Symbolic Life*, London: Routledge & Kegan Paul. (Collected Works of C.G. Jung, Vol. 18).

Kline, P. (1981) *Fact and Fantasy in Freudian Theory*, 2nd edn, London: Methuen.

Myers, I.B. and McCaulley, M.H. (1985) *Manual: A Guide to the Development and Use of the Myers-Briggs Type Indicator*, Palo Alto, Ca.: Consulting Psychologists Press.

Ornstein, R.E. (ed.) (1973) *The Nature of Human Consciousness*, San Francisco: Freeman.

—— (1977) *The Psychology of Consciousness*, 2nd edn, New York: Harcourt Brace Jovanovich.

Rachman, S.J. and Wilson, G.T. (1980) *The Effects of Psychological Therapy*, 2nd edn, Elmsford, NY: Pergamon Press.

Ryckman, R.M. (1985) *Theories of Personality*, 3rd edn, Monterey, Ca.: Brooks/Cole.

Samuels, A. (1985) *Jung and the Post-Jungians*, London: Routledge & Kegan Paul.

Schiff, B.B. and MacDonald, B. (1990) 'Facial asymmetries in the spontaneous response to positive and negative emotional arousal', *Neuropsychologia* 28, 8: 777–785.

Smith, M.L., Glass, G.V., and Miller, T.I. (1980) *The Benefits of Psychotherapy*, Baltimore: Johns Hopkins University Press.

Stein, M. (ed.) (1984) *Jungian Analysis*, London: Shambhala.

Stevens, A. (1982) *Archetype: A Natural History of the Self*, London: Routledge & Kegan Paul.

—— (1990) *On Jung*, London: Routledge.

Tucci, G. (1961) *The Theory and Practice of the Mandala*, London: Rider.

Von Franz, M.-L. (1964) 'The process of individuation', in C.G. Jung (ed.) *Man and His Symbols*, New York: Dell.

Wolff, W. (1933) 'The experimental study of forms of expression', *Character and Personality* 2: 168–176.

Wood, E. (1962) *Yoga*, Harmondsworth, Middlesex: Penguin Books.

Name index

Adam 22
Ames, L.B. 19
Anaxagoras 22
Annett, M. 19

Barsley, M. 19
Bradshaw, J.L. 25

Cirlot, J.E. 17, 27

Daniels, M. xii, 44
Dawson, E.R. 22

Eve 22

Freud, S. 4–5, 93

Gaia 22
Gesell, A. 19
Gimbutas, M. 21
Gurdjieff, G.I. 5

Isis 22

Jacobi, J. 14, 38–9, 42, 45, 47, 49, 93, 99
'Jane' 90–2, 97–8, 104–5
Jongbloet, P.H. 21
Jung, C.G. 4–5, 13–14, 27, 35, 37–42, 44–5, 47, 49, 51–6, 58, 61–2, 80, 82, 87–8, 93, 99–105, 109, 111–12, 116, 120, 135–6

McCaulley, M.H. 83, 88
MacDonald, B. 25
Myers, I.B. 83, 88

Nettleton, N.C. 25
Nuit 22

Ornstein, R.E. 25
Osiris 22

Pythagoras 22

Ra 22
'Rachel' 90–2, 95–7
Rachman, S.J. 5

St. Matthew 20
Samuels, A. 100
Satan 16
Schiff, B.B. 25
Smith, M.L. 5
Socrates 1
'Susan' 123–32

Tucci, G. 14

Von Franz, M.-L. 99

Wilson, G.T. 5
Wolff, W. 24
Wood, E. 16

Zeus 22

Subject index

ambiversion 62, 83, 85–6, 89–91, 94, 98, 104–5
amplification 93–4, 96–7, 110–11
analytical psychology 14, 38; see also Jungian psychology
androgyny 24; see also soul image
anima 37–9, 42, 99, 112, 120, 122, 136
animus 37–9, 42, 95–7, 99, 104–5, 128–9, 136
archetypes 42, 45, 58, 70, 108–11, 116, 133; and amplification 93–4; and individuation 99–104
attitude 54–6, 94; differentiation of 109, 126; inferior 55, 88, 99, 136; see also extraversion; introversion

backward, as symbol 15, 17, 26–7
Battle 28–31, 48–9, 97–8, 101–5, 110, 116, 119, 121, 129
Binah 23
birth control, and moon 21
body, sides of 24–6
brain 16–18, 25–6
Buddhism 4–5, 14, 70

Cabala 4, 23
calendar, lunar 21
centre, as symbol 14–15, 27
cerebral hemispheres 25–6, 28
chakras 17
Chokmah 23
Christianity 15, 20, 22–3, 26
circle, as symbol 14–15
comparing matrices 123–9
compensation 52–4, 88
complex 44, 93
composite matrices 129–32
consciousness 20, 23–5, 27–8, 34, 39, 43, 45–7; see also attitude; function
corpus callosum 25
counselling 4–7; and Watchword 107, 135
cross, as symbol 17, 26–7

day, principle of 20, 23–4
death 15, 20–1, 32, 50
Destiny 29–31, 35, 49–50, 97–8, 101–5, 110, 116–17, 119, 121, 129
development of self 98, 101–3, 105, 121, 129
developmental relationships 95, 98, 128; see also development of self; inner development; outer development
diagnosis 3; and Watchword 134–5
dialectical relationships 95–8, 117–19, 128
differentiation 42
direction see spatial metaphor
down, as symbol 15–17, 26–32
dreaming 4–5, 20–1, 25
Dwarf 28–32, 36–7, 46, 96–8, 110–12, 118–19

Earth Mother see Goddess cult
east, as symbol 20, 26–7
ego: ideals 36, 43–4; Jungian 47, 103–4
Egyptian mythology 22–3
emotion: and face 24–5; and feeling 52, 61; and handedness 19; and moon 21; and Soul 37–9
evil: and Shadow 44–5; and solar cult 19–23; and spatial metaphor 15–23; and Spectre 45–6

evolution, symbols of 16–17, 27
extraversion: defined 54–5; in matrix
    61–2, 94; and outer development
    100–1; symbols of 23–4; and
    unconscious 88, 136; *see also*
    feeling; intuition; sensation;
    thinking

face 24–5
feeling 51–4, 88, 90–2, 136; assessing
    61–2, 72, 75, 82–7; extraverted 59,
    77–9, 92; introverted 59–60, 80–2;
    repression of 58–9
female principle 20–4, 42, 99–100
folklore 15–16, 20–2
forward, as symbol 15, 17, 26–7
four, principle of 15, 26–7
free association 4–5, 93
function 51–4, 94; auxiliary 53, 82–3,
    88, 92, 109, 126, 132;
    differentiation of 109, 126; inferior
    52–3, 88, 99, 136; mixed 52–3,
    61–2, 82–7; *see also* feeling;
    intuition; sensation; thinking

gender *see* sex differences
gestalt therapy 5
Giant 28–32, 35–6, 96–7, 110–11,
    118–19, 124
God, gods 15–16, 19–24, 41, 70
Goddess cult 21–4, 42
Greek cross, as symbol 26–7
Greek mythology 15, 19–20, 22
Guide 28–31, 41–2, 95–100, 103,
    105, 110, 113, 117–18, 120, 128

hands, handedness 18–19, 23–5, 32
hemispheres *see* cerebral hemispheres
hero 22, 70, 116
horizontal dimension, symbolism of
    18–33
hypochondria 53, 58

ida 22
identification 40, 42
identity, identity crisis, 47, 101, 104,
    109–11, 115–16
illusion 57, 65
imagination 20–1, 24, 52–3
Imago 28–31, 35–6, 42–4, 96–9,
    103–4, 110, 113–14, 117–20 124,
    128
individuation: process 99–104;
    symbols of 14–15, 27, 35

initiation, into outward and inner
    reality 100, 103
inner development 44, 98–105,
    120–1, 128–9
inner principle 23–4, 27–32, 37–8,
    41–2, 44–5
integration *see* psyche
introversion: defined 54–5; and inner
    development 100–1; in matrix
    61–2, 94; symbols of 23–4; and
    unconscious 88, 136; *see also*
    feeling; intuition; sensation;
    thinking
intuition 41, 51–4, 88, 90–2, 136;
    assessing 60–2, 82–7; extraverted
    57–8, 65–9, 87; introverted 58,
    70–2, 92, 108–9; repression
    of 56–7
involution, symbols of 16–17, 27

Jungian analysis 4–5
Jungian psychology: criticisms 100–1;
    and symbols 14–15, 27, 116; and
    Watchword xii–xiii, 13–14, 35,
    102–4, 135; *see also* amplification;
    archetypes; ego; individuation;
    mana personality; *Persona*;
    psychological types;
    self-realization; *Shadow*; soul
    image; stages of life

keys: defined 28–31; described
    34–50; interpretation 94–5
king 21–2, 42
kundalini 16–17

language 15, 18, 25
left: handedness 18–19, 23–5;
    hemisphere 25–6; side of body
    24–5; side of matrix 28–33, 101; as
    symbol 18–27
life story 3–4, 7–8
lunacy 20–1
lunar cult 19–24, 42

madness *see* lunacy; psychosis
magic 20–1, 42
Magna Mater *see* Goddess cult
male: domination 21–3; principle
    21–4, 42, 99–100
mana personality 41–2, 99–100, 103,
    105, 113, 120
mandala 14–15
mask 39–40

maternal principle 20–1, 93
matriarchy 21
matrix: composite 129–32; procedure
    9–11; stabilities and change
    123–34; structure 13–15, 28–33
matter, principle of 17, 27, 42
maze, as symbol 116
meaning 3–4, 7
meditation 4–5
menstruation 20–2
mid-life crisis 100–1, 111, 120
moon *see* lunar cult
morality 16–17, 41, 48–9, 58, 104
Mount Olympus 15
Myers–Biggs Type Indicator 83
mysticism 58–60, 70
mythology 15–16, 20–2, 57, 94

narrative of life 3–4, 7–8, 95, 106
neurosis 55–60
night, principle of 20–4
north, as symbol 20, 26–7; North Star
    20

opposites: conjunction of 14–15, 27,
    29, 49, 103–4; in matrix 28–33;
    tables of 17, 22–3
other, role of 6–7, 33
outer development 44, 98–105,
    119–21, 128
outer principle 23, 27–32, 39–40,
    43–6
ovaries 22
Oxford English Dictionary 18

palmistry 24
patriarchy 21–3
Persona 28–31, 35, 39–40, 96–9, 101,
    103–4, 110, 112, 117–20, 127–8;
    Jungian 39–40, 103
personality: inner 31, 37–8, 47;
    integration 14, 39, 88; multiple 59;
    outer 31, 39–40, 47, 99; tests 1–3,
    134–5
pingala 22
polarity *see* opposites
progression, principle of 15–17,
    27–31, 35–6, 41–4, 48
projection 38–9, 44–6, 55–6, 60, 88,
    112, 114, 136
psyche, integration of 14, 29, 38–9,
    49, 88, 102–4
psychoanalysis 4–5, 25, 93, 133
psychological types 51–92, 108–9,

123, 126–7, 133–6; *see also*
    extraversion; feeling; introversion;
    intuition; sensation; thinking
psychosis 57
psychotherapy 4–7; and Watchword
    107, 135
pyramid, as symbol 17

rational-emotive therapy 5
regression, principle of 15–17, 27–31,
    36–7, 44–6, 48
relationships, analysing personal
    135–6; *see also* developmental
    relationships; dialectical
    relationships
religion 14–16, 19–23, 41, 58, 60, 70,
    92
repression 31, 39, 44–6, 52, 56–60
reversals, in matrix 32–3
right: handedness 18–19, 24–5;
    hemisphere 25–6; side of body
    24–5; side of matrix 28–33, 101; as
    symbol 18–27

schools, of self-development 5–7
self: dynamic 48, 102, 104; false 40,
    44; higher 41–2; idealized 43–4;
    inner 37–8; Jungian 49, 99, 103–4,
    116; public 39–40, 100, 112–13;
    real 38, 40; realized 31, 49, 102–4,
    116; sense of 46–7; static 46–8,
    101, 104
self-analysis 13, 107, 133–4
self-consciousness 5
self-deception 6–7, 107
self-development 6–7; *see also*
    development of self
self-knowledge 1–8, 33
self-observation 4–6
self-realization 14, 27, 49, 99–104,
    134
sensation 51–4, 88, 90–2, 136;
    assessing 60–2, 82–6; extraverted
    56, 62–4, 92; introverted 57, 65–7;
    repression of 57–8, 109, 121
sex differences 22–4, 42, 100; *see also*
    anima; animus; female principle;
    male principle; mana personality
Shadow 28–31, 44–6, 95–9, 103–4,
    110, 114–15, 117–18, 120, 128;
    Jungian 38, 44, 99, 103
Sky Father 22, 42
snake, as symbol 16–17
solar cult 19–24, 42

Soul 28–31, 37–9, 95–9, 101, 103–5, 110, 112, 117–18, 120, 128–9, 136
soul image 38–9, 99, 103; *see also* anima; animus; *Soul*
south, as symbol 26–7
spatial metaphor 14–33, 133
specialization, of brain function 25–6, 28
Spectre 28–31, 45–6, 96–9, 103–4, 110, 115, 117–19, 128
spine, as symbol 16–17, 22
spirit, spirituality 15–17, 27, 41–2; *see also* mana personality
spiritual traditions 4–7
split-brain studies 25
square, as symbol 14–15
stages of life 87–9, 99–104, 109, 120
Station 28–31, 46–7, 97–8, 101–5, 110, 115–16, 118–19, 121, 129
sun, as symbol 34–5; *see also* solar cult
symbol: in matrix 12, 34–50; and psychological integration 14, 27; spatial 14–33

testicles 22
tests 1–4; and Watchword 134–5
theme, of matrix 92, 109, 123–4, 127, 130, 134–6
therapy *see* psychotherapy
thinking 51–4, 88, 90–2, 136; assessing 61–2, 82–7; extraverted 58, 72–4; introverted 59, 75–7, 87–8; repression of 59–60
Titans 22

transactional analysis 5
tree, as symbol 16
triangle, as symbol 16–17
types *see* psychological types

unconscious: and *Guide* 41–2; and psychological types 52–5, 58, 88; and *Shadow* 44–5; and *Soul* 37–9; symbols of 20, 23–5, 27–8, 116; *see also* attitude; function; projection; repression
Underworld 15, 20
uniting symbol 14, 27
up, as symbol 15–17, 26–32

vertical dimension, symbolism of 15–17, 26–33

Watchword: applications 134–6; development of xii–xiii, 13–14; evaluation of xi, 13–14, 133–4; and Jung xii–xiii, 13, 102–4; purpose xii–xiii, 14; *see also* keys; matrix
west, as symbol 20, 26–7
Wise Old Man 42
witchcraft 22; *see also* magic
women's mysteries 20–2; *see also* female principle
word association, in matrix 9–11, 13, 28, 51, 95, 133; *see also* amplification; free association

Yggdrasil 16
yoga 16–17, 22